WHAT IS POSSIBLE NOW

WHAT IS POSSIBLE NOW

33 POLITICAL SITUATIONS

NAVID KERMANI

TRANSLATED BY TONY CRAWFORD

polity

Originally published in German as *Was jetzt möglich ist: 33 politische Situationen*
© Verlag C.H.Beck oHG, München 2022

This English edition © Polity Press, 2024

'The Dust on All the Faces' was originally published in German in *Die Zeit* no. 39, 2022. English translation by Tony Crawford published in *Plough Quarterly* no. 35, Spring 2023. Copyright © Tony Crawford.

Polity Press
65 Bridge Street
Cambridge CB2 1UR, UK

Polity Press
111 River Street
Hoboken, NJ 07030, USA

All rights reserved. Except for the quotation of short passages for the purpose of criticism and review, no part of this publication may be reproduced, stored in a retrieval system or transmitted, in any form or by any means, electronic, mechanical, photocopying, recording or otherwise, without the prior permission of the publisher.

ISBN-13: 978-1-5095-5763-9 (hardback)
ISBN-13: 978-1-5095-5764-6 (paperback)

A catalogue record for this book is available from the British Library.

Library of Congress Control Number: 2023936989

Typeset in 10.75 on 14pt Janson Text
by Cheshire Typesetting Ltd, Cuddington, Cheshire
Printed and bound in the UK by CPI Group (UK) Ltd, Croydon

The publisher has used its best endeavours to ensure that the URLs for external websites referred to in this book are correct and active at the time of going to press. However, the publisher has no responsibility for the websites and can make no guarantee that a site will remain live or that the content is or will remain appropriate.

Every effort has been made to trace all copyright holders, but if any have been overlooked the publisher will be pleased to include any necessary credits in any subsequent reprint or edition.

For further information on Polity, visit our website:
politybooks.com

Menge	Artikel	ASIN	UPC/EAN
1	Mollison's Blood Transfusion in Clinical Medicine (Klein, Mollison's Blood Transfusion in Clinical Medicine)	1405199407	9781405199407
1	Present Beyond Measure: Design, Visualize, and Deliver Data Stories That Inspire Action	1394202172	9781394202171
1	Anatomy and Physiology for Nursing and Healthcare Students at a Glance, 2nd Edition (Wiley Series on Cognitive Dynamic Systems)	1119757207	9781119757207

Amazon EU Société à responsabilité limitée, 5 Rue Plaetis, L-2338 Luxembourg, Registriert im Lux. RCS Nr B101818
Grundkapital: 37500, Lux. Handelsgesellschaft Nr 104408, Steuer Nr: 040 194 90837, UST-ID: DE 814584193
0/GhCJrVndL/-7 of 7-//AMZL-DHE6-ND/vendor-returns/0/0314-01:30/0313-06:49 Pack Type : F9
VRET**5598441360552

Contents

Preface viii

1 **Islam versus Islam** 1
   The Judgement against the Egyptian Quran Scholar Nasr Hamid Abu Zayd

2 **The Thousand Voices of Silence** 12
   The Situation of Artists and Intellectuals in Iran

3 **Sympathy for the Satan** 22
   After the Attacks of 11 September

4 **The Soft Words of Violence** 28
   After the Beginning of the War in Afghanistan

5 **What Alternative?** 34
   Before the War in Iraq

6 **Right Again, Sadly** 39
   The Attack on the Synagogue in Istanbul

7 **Strategy of Escalation** 45
   On the Hostages in Beslan

8 **A Good Thing You're Educating Me . . .** 49
   Confusion in the Integration Debate

9 **Desperation and Enthusiasm** 52
   After the French Referendum on the European Constitution

10 Hate Pictures and Hysteria 56
   The Dispute over the Muhammad Cartoons
11 Relying Only on Strength Makes Israel Weaker 62
   On the War in Lebanon
12 We Are Murat Kurnaz 68
   Before Foreign Minister Steinmeier's Testimony to the Bundestag Investigative Committee
13 The Message of Cologne 75
   The Discussion on Building a Grand Mosque
14 Death on Wednesday? 79
   The Trial of Ayatollah Boroujerdi in Tehran
15 Rejection of Europe 85
   The Swiss Referendum on the Prohibition of Minarets
16 A State without a People 91
   The Recent Mass Protests in Iran
17 Allianz Lecture on Europe 97
18 Triumph of Vulgar Rationalism 109
   The Outcry over Martin Mosebach and the Ban on Circumcision
19 Too Late for Good Conscience 114
   The Civil War in Syria
20 Farewell to the Middle East 119
   The 'Islamic State's' March on Baghdad
21 Stop the 'Islamic State'! 129
   The Threat of Genocide against Christians, Yazidis and other Ethnic Groups in Iraq
22 The European Ideal is Sinking 133
   The Mediterranean Sea as a Mass Grave
23 At Our Children's Cost 139
   Europe after Brexit

CONTENTS

24 What We Can Do in This Situation   149
After the Attacks in Ansbach, Würzburg and Munich

25 The Weight of Two Sacks   157
In Search of the Last Blind Spots of Progress in China

26 For Three Dollars a Day   167
After the West's Withdrawal from Afghanistan

27 No Programme but Politics   175
The Chancellorship of Angela Merkel

28 Afghanistan? Already a Non-Issue   182
German Apathy towards the World

29 The Price of Justice   191
The Disappearance of the Generic Masculine in German

30 War as a Means of Politics   204
After Vladimir Putin's Announcement of a Russian Troop Deployment to Donbas

31 Through the Night   211
Ukraine at War

32 The Dust on All the Faces   223
In South Madagascar, Farming Families Battle to Survive a Lethal Drought Caused by Climate Change

33 Woman, Life, Freedom   236
The Uprising in Iran, July–December 2022

Preface

Newspapers are ephemeral. The oldest of the essays I had planned to include in this book, the article on Nasr Hamid Abu Zayd which appeared in the *Frankfurter Rundschau* in 1993, was nowhere to be found at home, not even as a file on my computer. My editor wrote to the newspaper assuming they would have the article in their electronic archives – but in vain. All right, then they must have a basement where they archive the issues of years past, the editor supposed, and they could pull up the issue with the article for a suitable moderate fee. No, they didn't, the newspaper replied. *Frankfurter Rundschau*, until a few years ago one of the four, five national newspapers in the German-speaking countries with an outstanding cultural section and foreign reporting that, in sheer volume, seems almost unbelievable today – doesn't even have archives any longer. Finally, an assistant at the publishers' made the trip to the state library in Munich and found on a shelf the big, dust-covered binder with every issue of *Frankfurter Rundschau* from 1993. On opening it to 4 September, she had the presence of mind to take photos not only of the article we were looking for but of the front-page headlines too: 'Ukraine Relinquishes Nuclear Weapons – Accord Reached with Russia on Black Sea Fleet'. Thirty years later, in March of 2022, Ukraine was at war.

I started working for the Siegen local desk of the *Westfälische Rundschau* at the age of fifteen. From town council meetings to plays and rock concerts to demonstrations against the planned ring autobahn and the obligatory archery society fairs, there was nothing I would not cover. Since then I have continued to write for newspapers, more frequently in the beginning; more sporadically after my first books were published. What have I learned from the political situations that I described or analysed? If I had to pick out just one lesson, it would be this: I have learned, or, more precisely, I have experienced, seen with my own eyes, how single events that seem to be confined to one region can set off massive eruptions years later and far away. In politics, just as in nature, everything seems to be connected with everything else by chains of cause and effect whose complexity is impossible to foresee but often visible after the fact.

I remember how Afghan acquaintances told me in 1989 that it was actually Afghans who brought down the Berlin Wall. I was a student then, and their logic seemed a bit strained to me, but, when I studied the events in more detail, I soon realized that Mikhail Gorbachev's reform policies, the more immediate cause of the German unification, were causally connected with the Mujahidin's successful resistance against the Soviet Army – and hence with the Kremlin's 1979 decision to intervene militarily in Afghanistan. Another example: if the Democratic candidate Adlai Stevenson had been elected president of the United States in 1952, then the CIA would not have toppled the democratic Mosaddegh government in Tehran a year later, and there would have been no Islamic revolution in 1979 and no occupation of the American embassy – nor any of the further consequences in relations between the West and the Islamic world. And yet, during the election campaign, even Dwight D. Eisenhower probably hadn't thought much about Iran. And so on and so forth, down to the invasion of Ukraine: in 1993, that country relinquished its nuclear weapons only out of trust in the

Russian promise to respect its sovereignty and its existing borders. As the report on the front page of the *Frankfurter Rundschau* of 4 September 1993 indicates, Ukraine also demanded guarantees of its security from the West. I don't think anyone besides specialists in international relations still remembers that demand – I at least hadn't remembered it. Maybe it wasn't even taken seriously in the Western capitals at the time. But now, thirty years later, the whole world knows how reasonable the demand was. Fulfilling it then might well have prevented the present war, which is not only catastrophic for Ukraine, for Russia, for the whole of Europe, but will also result in terrible famines far away in East Africa. In the worst case, the refusal to guarantee Ukraine's security in 1993 may result in a third world war.

As I was compiling articles for the present book, the thought often crossed my mind that political decisions, which we may register as dubious although we cannot foresee their consequences, can have dramatic effects a long time later and in completely different places. Sometimes, however, the effects can also occur much more promptly – and then, strangely, everyone is just as surprised. Without the West's hasty withdrawal from Afghanistan, Russia would probably not have been tempted to attack Ukraine on the assumption that the West was divided, weary, anxious, busy with internal problems, and thus incapable of a resolute response. It was easy enough to guess that the images from Kabul airport, where Afghans clung in vain to the outsides of American aircraft, would be followed by further calamities, and not just for Afghanistan. I was not the only one to write that the Taliban's rule would make itself felt in the West as well – in the form of new migrations, cheaper drugs, retreats for terrorists, or further growth in China's power. But a war raging in the middle of Europe just a few months later? No, no one reckoned with that, except perhaps inside the Kremlin. And yet, in hindsight, a connection can be seen reaching from the Soviet Army's invasion of Afghanistan in 1979 to the rise of Islamic fundamentalism and the 9/11 attacks, to America's wars in the Middle East, the passiveness of the West in Syria and the refugee crisis of 2015, and finally to Brexit, Trump and the West's weakness, resulting in the increasingly confident actions of China and Russia. Similar threads run through every area of our social lives; but we don't realize it when we open today's newspapers, and much less if we only follow TV news or click on the top headlines online. Just think of climate change, which is mainly caused by us in the North and results in severe droughts in the South, and consequently in wars breaking out and whole populations losing their livelihoods – if not the physical ground under their feet, as in Bangladesh or in the Maldives. What an illusion it is to think that we could be shielded from the developments all around us on this ever-shrinking planet – and how sobering to see that the illusion is cultivated afresh every four years in electoral campaigns that centre on nothing but Germany, Germany, Germany.

The present book is not a representative or authoritative survey of the major political developments of the past three decades, and that is not only because the issues I am able to comment on are inevitably limited. Furthermore, as I have already hinted, I wrote for newspapers more often in some years and then rarely in others because books, and sometimes life, monopolized my time. And up until the pandemic, a large part of my journalistic work consisted of travel writing. As talk shows and the internet have advanced the inflation of everybody's opinions on everything, my urge to report from abroad has grown steadily stronger. But although many of my travel texts first appeared in newspapers, almost all of them have also been collected and published as complete books. I have also left aside the cultural commentary, critical reviews and literary impressions I have published in newspapers over the years: this book is limited to my political statements. Of those, I have selected the thirty-three that seem most significant to me from the vantage point of the present, whether because they evoked the strongest reactions immediately upon publication, or because they are still relevant today, or subsequent developments have made them relevant again. I have also included certain articles that were collected in earlier books in German: in the anthology *Strategie der Eskalation: Der Nabe Osten und die Politik des Westens* [Strategy of escalation: the Middle East and Western policy], in the essay *Wer ist Wir? Deutschland und seine Muslime* [Who is 'we'? Germany and its Muslims], and in modified versions in the novel *Dein Name*.

Not all of my predictions have turned out to be correct, and the present book does not hide the miscalculations I have made. The present-day reader looking back on the situations I wrote about will rest his or her own judgement on a foundation that is more solid for the time that has passed. On reviewing the texts, however, I was dismayed to see that my hopes were seldom borne out but my fears often were, or else exceeded. And so one of the lessons that I have learned, as a political commentator and still more as a reporter, is, sadly, this: violence works. Those who mercilessly persecute their political opponents, deploying firearms against peaceful demonstrators from the moment protests begin or dropping bombs on an insurgent population, have a good chance of holding on to power. It is not glasnost that set an example in the watershed year of 1989, but Tiananmen. In a way, the same can be said of our Western democracies, whether in the United States, Europe or Israel: violating international law, taking a hard line in combating terror, abandoning the rule of law, inciting hostility against migrants, or redefining democracy as a dictatorship of the majority are all too often the way to win the next election.

Violence works. But for how long? If in politics as in nature everything is connected with everything else by chains of cause and effect, violence must sooner or later catch up with the perpetrators, or at least with their descendants, their societies. For that reason it is wrong, no matter what the political situation, to let one's own actions be guided by promises of short-term success, minimal commitment, or momentary popularity. Nothing has caused as much real-political damage since the Second World War as so-called *Realpolitik*. It is not merely morality's doing if our religions revere not the selfish but the martyrs and, even in our present-day secular societies, those heroes who rebel against injustice. Looking beyond the single day that is recorded in a given issue of a newspaper, it is also better from the point of view of self-preservation.

Cologne, May 2022

1

ISLAM VERSUS ISLAM

The Judgement against the Egyptian Quran Scholar Nasr Hamid Abu Zayd

Frankfurter Rundschau, 4 September 1993

Ebtehal Yunes found out about her impending divorce in the newspaper. An industrious and zealously religious Egyptian lawyer had requested the divorce from a duly convened Egyptian court – unbeknownst to her and her husband, the lecturer Nasr Hamid Abu Zayd. The grounds: the marriage of a Muslim woman with an apostate is, he argued, invalid under Islamic law.

A joke in poor taste, one might think, but in fact it is the latest high point in an affair that has kept the Egyptian public in suspense for months. The *Washington Post* thought the controversy, which centres on some of the Egyptian scholar's books on literature and Islamic studies, was important enough to be reported on its front page. For good reason: the misery of the Muslim world and the desperate struggle for reform appear here in condensed form, as if under a microscope. 'I expected the worst,' Ms Yunes is quoted in the *Washington Post*. If the court orders the divorce, she plans to leave the country with her husband: 'Do you know of any other solution? We are not heroes.'

Nasr Hamid Abu Zayd's books deal with the Quran and the

history of Islamic theology – and he is finding out first-hand what a touchy subject that is in today's Egypt. A majority of Abu Zayd's studies are published abroad; his appointment as professor at Cairo University was refused on flimsy grounds; the centre of Sunni Islamic theology, Azhar University in Cairo, has charged him with apostasy; he is treated with abject abuse in the press; preachers publicly denounce him as a heretic; death threats land in his letterbox; by his own account he and his family are being terrorized; there is a lawsuit to divorce him from his wife; and now a lawyer declares him fair game: 'Our constitution protects the rights of members of all three religions, Christianity, Islam and Judaism. But it does not protect those who decide to abandon their religion,' Muhammad Samida Abu Samada tells the *Middle East Times*, explaining why it seemed unavoidable to him to request the divorce of the Abu Zayd couple.

At about the same time, Sheikh Muhammad Ghazali, one of Egypt's most influential theologians, who until recently was considered a moderate, spoke out in favour of murdering 'apostates' if the state does not fulfil its obligation to condemn and punish the blasphemers. Ghazali, known even in the remotest villages through his regular television appearances, promulgated this carte blanche for vigilante justice in his testimony for the defence at the trial of thirteen fanatics charged with murdering the secularist author Farag Foda. Foda was shot in front of his house in 1992 after having been branded a heretic – like Abu Zayd – in the loyalist press. The Egyptians understood quite clearly that the respected sheikh was practically legalizing murdering Abu Zayd. What had begun barely three years before with the publication of a literary study of the Quran may end with the exile, if not the death, of its author. 'There is no discussion with you,' read one of the anonymous letters. 'All that matters is that you emigrate to some place far away from the Islamic world, because you won't be able to live in a country that you are trying to destroy. No matter how the police try to protect you, you will not escape.'

Is this the standard procedure? After Salman Rushdie, Aziz Nesin, Sadiq al-Azm, Muhammad Khalafallah, Said al-Ashmawi, Mahmoud Mohammed Taha, is another advocate of Western secular Enlightenment being threatened by religious terrorists? Is it further evidence of a rise in religiously motivated intolerance in the Islamic world? Or another sign of the Muslims' clash with modernism, now being waged against the modernists in their own ranks?

Let's not rush to simple answers. Most of the authors I listed are not primarily advocates of the Western ideals of freedom and human rights – although they are often so portrayed – but products of their own Middle Eastern and Islamic culture, just as much as the great simplifiers in the fundamentalist camp are. The conflict is not between modernists influenced by the West on the one hand and fundamentalists bound to their tradition on the other: rather, both currents, each of them infinitely diverse and disunited, have their roots in the same culture, one that is deeply and irreversibly shaped by the West. The conflict is not between two cultures, each with its own different values, but between two positions within one culture. Khomeini no more represents Islam than Rushdie does the values of the West; rather, both of them stand, in the same intellectual world, for different answers to its unmistakable crisis. The case of Abu Zayd illustrates that a genuine modernist of Islamic culture can be much more traditionalistic than all the traditionalists.

The debate over the Cairo scholar Abu Zayd, which later expanded to call his other works into question, was sparked by the publication of *Mafhum an-Nass* (roughly, 'The concept of text'), in which he examines the Quranic revelation using the methods of literary analysis and linguistics. The book's stated goal is to create an awareness of the historicity of the text and the dialectical relationship between revelation and reality. To this end, it meticulously shows both how very much the Quran is conditioned by the cultural and historic context in which it was revealed and how it happened that this fact, which should be self-evident, became taboo as Islamic theology evolved, so that the Quran was ultimately surrounded by an aura of untouchability. God's message, Zayd wrote, has been degraded 'to a reified, sacred object' and 'an object of ornamentation'.

One must be conscious of the paramount position of the Quran in the Islamic faith to understand the uproar caused by Abu Zayd's scholarly approach. To highlight that position, I may recall that the Quran in Islamic doctrine holds the central function that is reserved in Christianity to the very person of Jesus Christ: that is, it does not simply proclaim God but is itself divine in nature. Although not one line of his book denies the divine origin of the Quran, Abu Zayd excludes that matter from the scholarly discourse. What can be studied, just as any other text – i.e., a literary text – can be studied, is not the divine nature of the text but only its significance as a document which came into being in reality, which reflects influences of that reality, and which in turn changes that reality. 'I treat the Quran as a text in the Arabic language which both Muslims and Christians – or atheists – should study because it contains a condensation of Arab culture and because its resonance is still found in other texts in that culture,' Abu Zayd said in a conversation I had with him last year. 'It is a text which assimilated the pre-Islamic texts and which has been assimilated by all the texts that have come after it, even those being written today.'

In fact, Abu Zayd's analytical Quran exegesis recalls in several respects historical-critical Bible research, whose methods were as revolutionary for Christian theology as the work of the Cairo scholar seems to be for Islam – and which many Christians still see as 'degeneracy in religion', to use the Egyptian press's characterization of Abu Zayd's position. A crucial difference, however, is this: while historical-critical Bible research was a completely new way of relating to the revealed scripture, the same cannot be said of Abu Zayd. Besides the fact that other Muslim authors have put forth similar approaches in recent decades, Nasr Hamid Abu Zayd is well within the tradition of classical Islamic scholarship. What is more, in his striving for scientific rigour in Quran exegesis, Abu Zayd appeals again and again to tradition – or, more precisely, to the text-critical methods of classical Islamic theology. In my conversation with him, he characterized this approach very distinctly: 'We must study the Quran the same way we study the language of Shakespeare, with the tools and the methods of linguistic analysis, to discover its meaning. That is how the scholars used to study it.'

But why the turmoil if what Abu Zayd is advocating is, in principle, nothing new? The Egyptian public was reacting not to Abu Zayd's references to progressive and pluralistic elements in the early tradition but to his critique of a Quran interpretation which emerged in the tenth century and which dominates the theological discourse today. Abu Zayd calls that interpretation reactionary. It isolates the Quran from the context of its objective historical circumstances, thus distorting its message and its meaning for society. And, Abu Zayd continues, there are political reasons for this: rationality, anti-dogmatism and diversity in Quran exegesis have been lost since the theologians fell under the sway of the state, which by nature wants to solidify the status quo. The preservation and monopolization of Quran interpretation by 'state theologians' has contributed to the conservation of existing conditions by branding new interpretations and critical questions, which are often charged with volatile social implications, as heretical and exposing their proponents to persecution.

Abu Zayd's problem is that the religious discourse he criticizes is often equated today with Islam itself. Opposition to a certain theological current becomes an 'attack on the Quran and the Sunnah', as *Al-Alamout al-Islami*, the most influential mouthpiece of the Muslim World League, published in Riyadh, claims. It becomes apparent that a good Muslim today must believe not only in God and His messenger but also in the quasi-official scholars preaching on television. A third proposition is added to Islam's twofold profession of faith: the belief in an Islamic church, a thing prohibited in Islam which has practically become established nonetheless in many Muslim countries.

Abu Zayd's attack on the state-aligned theologians, his challenge to their monopoly on the interpretation of the scriptures, has considerable importance for current political affairs. It is a manifestation of numerous intellectuals' struggle against the growing influence of the Islamists in all areas of society and the increasing public acceptance of radical ideas. Abu Zayd is unmasking a phenomenon which can also be observed in Germany today in the treatment of far-right parties: the governing parties fight the extremist organizations, but at the same time adopt their political programme. Because Abu Zayd's criticism of social developments appears in the context of Islamic studies, it is no wonder that those he criticizes and their apologists respond with the accusation – a life-threatening one in Egypt today – of apostasy.

The aggressive reactions to the publication of *Mafhum an-Nass* have not kept Abu Zayd from pursuing and detailing his attack on state-sponsored Islam in other books and articles. In the 1992 work *Critique of Religious Discourse*, for example, he accuses the official religious institutions of failing to distinguish themselves in substance from the militant Islamist opposition. 'The only difference between them', Abu Zayd told me, 'is that the extremists know the political import of these ideas and are trying to change the society. The dispute arises only over the political meaning of the ideas; the intellectual foundations are the same. How can the official religious media serve such a distorting function?'

The skewing effect of the Egyptian media is dramatically evident in the debate on Abu Zayd. An article by Abdul-Galil Shalaby in the government-aligned newspaper *Al-Gomhuria*, for example, leads the uninformed reader to assume that Abu Zayd attributes Muhammad's emergence to economic causes – although there is not a word to that effect in the book. Fahmi Huwaidi, a columnist for the state newspaper *Al-Ahram*, diagnoses Abu Zayd as having a personal aversion to Islam and its prophet; the popular author Mustafa Mahmud complains in the same newspaper that Abu Zayd considers transcendence purely mythical; and Jamal Badawi, editor in chief of the formerly liberal *Al-Wafd*, is indignant that Abu Zayd abuses his academic freedom to wilfully denigrate the religion. They concur with the president of the Egyptian Writers' Union, Tharwat Abaza, who announces, 'There is no doubt: he is an unbeliever.'

Such claims – libellous though they may be – have to be taken seriously, just as the murder of Farag Foda, the intimidation of Said Ashmawi, and the condemnation of Salman Rushdie have been taken seriously. These are not flyers printed by an extremist organization but newspaper articles by men occupying the top positions in the Egyptian media. They are upstanding citizens and at the same time demagogues. They are declaring open season on Abu Zayd. The extremist organizations don't need to hand out flyers if what they are saying is printed in the state publications of the United States' closest ally in the Middle East. All they need to do is carry it out.

The scandal over Cairo University's refusal to promote Abu Zayd to professor casts a light on the increasing influence of Islamist ideas in the former bastions of secular scholarship. In May of last year, the lecturer in Rhetorical and Islamic Studies, who had previously taught in Japan and the United States, presented his candidacy for habilitation, supported by two books and thirteen articles. Of the three evaluators, two approved the submission, while the third, Professor Abd al-Sabur Shahin, rejected it in a polemical, rudely worded statement. Shahin, a prominent member of the governing National Democratic Party, found that, in addition to monstrous lies, Abu Zayd's works contained substantive errors, perverse and Marxist-atheistic ideas and 'the most abhorrent contempt for the principles of the faith', and condescendingly recommended that he disseminate his ideas only in literary journals with low circulation in order to avoid incurring the society's wrath.

When, after a heated debate, the thirteen-person selection committee ignored the two positive evaluations and rejected Abu Zayd's habilitation, his colleagues at the university and other intellectuals and journalists responded with dismay and tried to challenge the committee's decision. To their surprise, however, many newspapers sided with Shahin. When the university definitively rejected Abu Zayd's habilitation on 18 March, even the Egyptian human rights commission intervened, condemning the academic senate's decision as 'an attack on freedom of conscience, freedom of speech, and scientific research in Egypt'. The magazine *Ruz al-Yusuf* called the university's decision 'a scientific and academic disgrace', while the left-leaning weekly *Al-Ahali* ran the headline 'Terrorism Threatens Major Bastion of Thought'. Ghali Shukri wrote in his weekly column in *Al-Ahram* that Cairo University had become a 'court of the Inquisition and a centre of terrorism'. Lutfi al-Khuli argued similarly in the

English-language *Al-Ahram Weekly*, demanding a national debate on the state of the universities 'because we are now beginning to see alarming evidence – both in the universities and elsewhere – of the danger of suppression of intellectual activities, the compulsive uniformity of academic work and the liquidation – whether physical, by bullets, or only metaphoric – of thinkers and authors who are accused of blasphemy. In other words, the terrorism in the streets has begun to spread in the universities, and vice versa.'

'A Quran that is neither read nor understood is a book like any other, an unwritten page,' Ali Shariati told his listeners in Tehran in the early seventies. 'That is why they go to such trouble to keep us from reading it, understanding it, thinking about it. They say we wouldn't understand it because it's so complicated; they forbid all rational interpretation of it.' Shariati was murdered in 1977, probably not by Islamic fundamentalists but by the Iranian shah's henchmen. In today's Iran too there is no place for many of his books, and his widow once said that, if her husband were still alive, he would surely be in prison.

Nasr Hamid Abu Zayd's lasting achievement is that he did not describe the plight of Arab culture by outward comparisons but penetrated straight to the core of that culture to expose the sclerosis that has set in around its heart: the Quran. Regardless of what may happen to him now – whether he gets shot or driven into exile – a new Abu Zayd will come after him. They will arise again and again, in very different forms – modernists and reformers, blasphemers and heretics, Iqbals and al-Afghanis, Ashmawis and Fodas, Rushdies and Abu Zayds; they will not disappear until Islamic culture finds a way out of the intellectual and social destitution it is suffering. Like fundamentalism and traditionalism, they are a reflex, a necessary response to the challenge of the modern age. 'As long as no pre-scientific system of belief and method of assimilating the world and acting in it has the ability to resist the penetration and disruption of the modern scientific system, future Rushdies will continue to turn up, with a regularity approaching that of the laws of physics, in the Islamic world,' wrote the Syrian Sadiq al-Azm in the debate on the *Satanic Verses*.

You can think what you like about modern society, and for the Middle East in particular there are plenty of reasons to approach it with distrust and caution – but you cannot escape it. How sad it is, and how distressing, that the most creative and intelligent, the most respectable and courageous minds in the Islamic world – scientists, theologians and artists – are being slandered and antagonized, ostracized and murdered by their own social milieu. It is they who are upholding their culture and their identity in a changed world instead of timidly seeking refuge in dogmas and ignorance. They are contending with modernism instead of running away from it. They are working to find answers instead of burying their heads in the sand. They will not be silenced. We should listen to them and not just to the blowhards wielding the alleged Sword of Islam.

But the Abu Zayd affair also offers reasons to hope. A society that can produce such self-critical books cannot be utterly finished. The outcry they evoke is also an indication that they are touching a nerve. And the reactions have by no means been all negative. Thanks to Abu Zayd, many people, and in particular many of his students, have mustered the courage to question what has long been proclaimed to them as indisputable. They have learned that the Islamic tradition encompasses many progressive and pluralistic impulses. A discussion has begun. Insults and threats have set off a wave of solidarity that is not limited to Egypt.

At the same time, the attacks on Nasr Hamid Abu Zayd have revealed the unscrupulous methods with which the

Islamic discourse is being carried on. An argument built on such shaky footing will not be able to stand for long – that is the hope, desperate as it is. Perhaps the often discussed advance of fundamentalism is in fact a bitterly fought defensive battle against the incursion of reality in people's consciousness. And the incontestable danger of fundamentalism is perhaps that of a wounded animal. 'My considered opinion', Sadiq al-Azm writes, 'is that it is becoming increasingly clear in the Muslim societies that the price of a decision *against* the modern system of scientific logic, of faith, of comprehending the world and acting in it, is consigning ourselves to the dustbin of history.' If Islamic culture escapes this fate, it will have scholars such as Nasr Hamid Abu Zayd to thank for it.

2

THE THOUSAND VOICES OF SILENCE

The Situation of Artists and Intellectuals in Iran
Süddeutsche Zeitung, 12 August 1995

A *Stammtisch* is a German pub table where the same locals always meet, on the same day of the week or month, over decades. If there was such a place in Tehran, it would be around Imam Hussein Square. Picking this area to begin a report on artists and intellectuals in Iran is like going to the Bavarian foothills of the Alps to report on Germany's techno scene. The square is at the midpoint of a plebeian area, a district of small merchants, workers and tradesmen, loud, lively and deeply religious. Nowhere in the city is the popular Shiite religion, with its rituals, traditions and customs, as visible as in this square and in the surrounding streets and lanes. The only cultural institutions you would expect to find here are tea houses, Shiite passion plays and cinemas showing Iranian Rambo knock-offs.

'This area is dingier than a dead dog,' grumbles the taxi driver from the genteel north of Tehran as I guide him into a side street. But here is where the editorial offices of *Gardun* are located, one of Iran's most progressive cultural magazines. In the top storey of a little block of flats, people not only discuss the latest book on French deconstructivism or the new film by Wim Wenders; this is also a staging area of the struggle for free speech in the Islamic Republic. In recent years, many critical articles and books have been disseminated from here; authors have argued for the revival of the Iranian Writers' Association, strongly supported the sensational protest declaration published by 134 Iranian writers last autumn, and campaigned for the writer Saidi Sirjani, who died in prison – probably murdered – in January. As I enter the four-room flat that serves as both editorial and production offices, I realize: this is where a report on the life of artists and intellectuals in the Islamic Republic must begin. The restrictions they are subjected to, and at the same time the persistence of their efforts, could not be more tangible anywhere than in these rooms decorated with artists' portraits and theatre posters from all over the world.

With a circulation of 20,000 to 25,000, *Gardun* is one of Iran's most read cultural magazines. And yet – in spite of extreme austerity in its staff costs and rudimentary equipment (there's not even a fax machine) – the paper doesn't come close to breaking even. That is mainly because it no longer receives a contingent of subsidized paper. The result: *Gardun* has to buy paper on the open market, at a price eight times higher. That makes every issue a losing venture from its inception. Another way in which the state deals with insubordinate minds: private companies are given to understand that it is better not to advertise in magazines like *Gardun*. Accordingly, the copy of the journal that the publisher Abbas Maroufi hands me to read, fresh off the press, contains no advertising at all. Although in recent years Maroufi was repeatedly able to finance the magazine using the money earned by his novels and stories, which enjoyed large print runs in the Iranian market, this source of revenue has dried up too: Maroufi is not allowed to reissue any of his books, much less publish a new novel.

'What else will they prohibit?' asks Esmail Jamshidi, an editor at *Gardun*. 'We're practically closed down. If we bring out just two issues instead of the fourteen we planned, the magazine really doesn't exist any more. How can we keep our readers, our subscribers?' And Abbas Maroufi recently wrote in his editorial, addressing a section head in the ministry of culture: 'We spend more than half of our time exposing your swindles, and the rest of the time we are held hostage by you, the paper suppliers, the banks and a crust of bread. We cut off a piece of our sleep and our soul in order to write something. A piece of a soul that is already wounded and half dead. And now, as I write this, I realize that, as far as my books are concerned in this country, I can recite the prayer for the dead. And I recite it.'

Maroufi is a lean man in his mid-thirties with a moustache and dark, piercing eyes, restless, full of plans, and with the emotion of one fighting for a better world. He doesn't want to give up, to withdraw into literature. 'Intellectuals in every age have spent their blood,' he says. 'Look at the life of André Malraux. People like that really slogged. Or Camus, Sartre, who sacrificed themselves for their cause. How many deaths did they die; how often were they flayed alive? You can't just sit in a corner and write novels, least of all in Iran.'

That may sound old-fashioned. But when you're dealing with Iranian artists and intellectuals, you sometimes feel you've been sent back in time to the 'fabulous' days when art was the expression of an immediate affliction and, at the same time, the most subversive form of rebellion. There may have been a similar effect in the communist or Latin American military dictatorships. What else besides art's necessity in the face of a shocking reality can explain the fact that, in the Islamic Republic of Iran of all countries, ambitious auteur films are made and classical Iranian music continues to evolve, avant-garde poetry and big novels of social criticism are written, and dozens of notable cultural journals are published? Iranian films have won more than 170 awards at international festivals in recent years, from Cannes to Berlin, Tokyo and Montreal. Concerts by Iranian and international ensembles sell out months in advance. The country's conservatories are booming. After some three thousand new book titles appeared each year in pre-revolutionary Iran, today there are ten thousand, some of them selling hundreds of thousands of copies. Many of the new titles are translated from European languages. Because private poetry readings are among the most popular leisure-time activities, an Iranian newspaper ran the headline a few months ago, alluding to the country's bottomed-out economy: 'Iran Holds World Record – in Poem Production'.

It is not only the political pressure that drives many people to give artistic expression to their distress and their fears. In the past sixteen years, the Iranians have been subjected to what must be a unique concentration of historic events and changes: a revolution, an eight-year war, natural disasters such as the 1990 earthquake which killed more than sixty thousand people, an economic crisis that is threatening the livelihoods of whole segments of the population, and streams of migrants leaving the country and entering it, bleeding Iran financially and intellectually and at the same time making it the country with the most refugees in the world.

Yet the population's formative experience may have been something else: the collective boundary experience of the Iranian society; the experience of death and the despair at its senselessness. At demonstrations and on the battlefield, many people have looked death in the face with their own eyes, and the omnipresence of death is further heightened by the cult of penitence and martyrdom in popular Shiite religion. Practically every family has martyrs to mourn – martyrs of the revolution, martyrs of the war, martyrs of the resistance against the mullahs' regime. And for what? Most people are neither better off nor freer today than they were twenty years ago. All the blood for nothing; the sacrifices for nothing; the running, fighting, living – for nothing: that is the experience that has formed many Iranians' outlook on life.

And there is no end to the running. There is no rest and no catching their breath. Today it is the daily race for a living; two, three jobs in parallel, fourteen hours a day, six and a half days a week: that is the workaday life of many Iranians. 'Is that what the people fought a revolution for?' Abbas Maroufi asked some time ago in an editorial: 'For the idea of freedom to extinguish itself; for the day's twenty-four hours to run out before they have a chance just to say the word freedom?'

Many Iranians withdraw into private life or flee, finances permitting, into consumption. Satellite TV, video, cheap Western culture, all are booming. Others become poets. Art is a way for many Iranians to deal with the vanity of human striving. It gives expression to the questioning, the bewilderment, the despair, the betrayed hope for a better future. It proclaims, as the great Iranian storyteller Mahmoud Dowlatabadi once said, 'with a thousand voices of silence: I am mute.'

It has often been noted at international film festivals that the Iranian contributions share a seriousness, a depth, an absoluteness, even when they are comedies. The reason – of course – is the reality which confronts filmmakers in Iran. What is expressed in the artists' work, the experiences of a society, is significantly more brutal, and more existential for the individual, than in Western Europe. I do not want to glorify anyone: in Iran too there is a great deal of mediocrity and art-as-entertainment. During my stay, however, I have met a few people who impressed me so greatly that I thought: these people are heroes. They exploit every bit of leeway the system leaves them, pushing against its boundaries again and again to move them inch by inch.

It is often hard to see from the outside where those boundaries lie. To those affected by them, however, they are usually very plain. 'Can you say that out loud?' I ask an older professor of literature who has just described to me in no uncertain terms the disastrous consequences of Iranian educational policy.

'I even publish articles on this topic,' replies the professor, who is among the most respected scholars in the country. 'I can't sit still when I see that we are heading for the abyss.'

'And you don't get in trouble?'

'Ah! I'm one of the dinosaurs here; they leave me in peace; we're dying out anyway. If they fired me, it would do them more harm than letting me complain a little now and then. Almost all of the former elite of Iranian scholars is already gone. Emigrated or fired. The academic level has sunk so low, especially in the social sciences, that they've begun making efforts to keep the rest here. So, where I work, I can say what I think. But a young assistant professor, a doctoral candidate or an undergraduate could never say it publicly without getting thrown out of the university.'

There it is: a boundary. In this case, it divides a seventy-year-old literature professor who rose to fame through his publications under the shah from the younger generation of academics. To be pulled down from a pedestal, it takes more than a few critical words. To climb up onto the pedestal, you have to be perfectly streamlined – in speech, in print and in outward appearance. 'In ordinary lectures, I have all kinds of students in front of me; the typical Hisbollahis are rather the exception. But when I look around in the graduate-level courses, I see almost nothing but unshaven men and chador-wearing women. Their greatest academic talent is grovelling.

Those are the criteria by which the elites are selected here. What can we expect for the future of a country with an elite like that?'

I ask the professor whether I can interview him for a German newspaper, and I run up against a second boundary. 'Certainly – as long as you don't mention my name.'

'But you said you have the luxury of criticizing the state publicly.'

'Yes, but it stays within the country. If my name suddenly turns up in a Western newspaper, they can give me trouble. My reputation and my age won't help me then. That would be outside the boundaries within which I can act.'

The boundary between private and public expression is fairly clear. Insults, curses and sarcasm against the rulers are heard practically everywhere: in taxis, in the street, even in government offices, schools and universities; sometimes shouted and sometimes in whispered asides. Thus, in the private sphere, there is in fact freedom of opinion. Art, on the other hand, is subject to strict censorship. Among the many paradoxes of Iranian reality is this, however: censored writers can complain about this censorship in independent periodicals. This is because periodicals, if they are not banned outright, are hardly inspected before publication – unlike novels and screenplays. Thus there is also a boundary that divides artistic and journalistic expression. Art, the word of the poet, is kept under much more severe control – no wonder in a country where poetry is almost a staple. 'We have always lived with censorship and political pressure, under the shah too,' says the poet Mohammed-Ali Sepanlou, who was one of the founding members of the Iranian Writers' Association in the late sixties. 'We have never been free. But we have always had something to say. Our hope is to be free one day and still to have something to say when that day comes.'

Now Sepanlou is among those who are still allowed to publish a book now and then. And, if not, he can at least sit at home and write. Other artists are denied even this option. When I talk with the film director Bahram Beyzai about the vitality and power of Iranian art, for example, he tells me, 'What reaches the market is only a fraction of what would be possible.' And he adds that art has been hit in the face until it is half dead and wheezing. What looks to me like vitality is really a wounded groaning.

Bahram Beyzai is the grand old man of Iranian cinema. What he has done for Iranian culture – with his films, his books and his plays, and as a university professor – is unparalleled. He made a name for himself in Europe mainly with his film *Bashu, the Little Stranger*, shot in 1986 but released by the Iranian authorities only three years later, which won numerous prizes and was shown on television several times. I visited Beyzai in Tehran. The afternoon I spent in his home is one of the saddest experiences of my trip to Iran.

Beyzai lives outside the city limits in a squalid suburb. There, in the converted basement of his parents' home, one of the most important directors in the history of Iranian cinema leads his existence, an artist as famous in Iran as Louis Malle is in Europe. Nearly sixty years old, he lives in the basement together with his wife, an actor. Beyzai's artistic production has come almost to a complete halt. He has not been allowed to make films for five years or to direct plays for the past fifteen years. He was dismissed from his post as professor at the film academy – because of his Baha'i family background – in the early 1980s. All that is left him is writing. Beyzai is permitted to publish here and there, but not enough to live on; furthermore, his books, when they are printed at all, are heavily censored. Even his plays that are published in print are not allowed to be produced by Iranian theatre ensembles. 'Every artist in Iran is a hostage,' Beyzai complains. 'If someone shoots a film the government doesn't like, they simply don't get a permit next time. That is easier and more effective than holding a trial.' The reason Beyzai can no longer make films is that he protested against the censorship of his film *Travellers*. Since then, he hasn't had a chance with the censors.

But Beyzai tells me something else as well. Some years ago he visited Europe. Several television networks, including the German public network ZDF, expressed interest in producing a film by the Iranian director. But the German network had a condition: no criticism of the Islamic Republic. Beyzai went back to Iran without a deal. 'I wasn't planning on making a political film, but if they're going to make that a condition right from the start, I can't sign. I haven't seen stipulations like that even in Iran.'

Complaints about the West's attitude are not rare among Iranian intellectuals and artists. The scepticism grounded in the historical experience with the West during the shah's rule, the revolution and the first Gulf War is now augmented by the feeling of being punished for things they can't prevent. The cultural boycott decreed in the course of the Salman Rushdie affair isolates Iranian artists from the rest of the world. And it benefits those factions in Iran that would like to see cooperation with the West limited to technology and trade anyway. None of the Iranian artists I met supported Khomeini's fatwa. But all of them perceived the affair as an instrument of Western governments: a painless way of demonstrating a resolute stance for human rights to their own populations without endangering their wonderful business relationships. And yet a dialogue with artists and intellectuals as the representatives of a different Iran would be much more than a gesture of solidarity. Engaging with their life experiences is worth while because of the quality of their works.

On the day before my departure, I visit the offices of *Gardun* once more. On Maroufi's desk I see a brand-new fax machine. A high official in the Post and Telecommunications Ministry arranged for the editors to receive it. In addition, a few advertisements have been sold, and – still more importantly – Maroufi's new book has received the imprimatur. The same evening, I hear by telephone that the literature professor who thought he was untouchable in spite of his acerbic criticism of educational policy has been fired. He seems to have miscalculated the boundary. Hope and fear on the same day.

In Isfahan I met a well-known Iranian lutenist who told me Iranian music is like a dough. 'The bureaucrats and the mullahs have the dough in their hands,' he said. 'They want to keep it as small as possible, so they squeeze it with their fingers as tight as they can. But the more they squeeze it, the firmer it gets. Let them squeeze. Let them try and crush the dough. It will only get firmer, and it squirts out of the gaps between their fingers.' And then the musician cried, 'Tell that to the Europeans! Tell them how we're living here, and that the dough is very firm by now.'

3

SYMPATHY FOR THE SATAN

After the Attacks of 11 September

Süddeutsche Zeitung, 18 September 2001

It is hardly remarkable in itself that football teams all over the world observed a minute's silence for the victims of the attacks in New York and Washington. It is remarkable that they did the same in Tehran at the qualification match between the national teams of Iran and Bahrain. In the very capital of the Islamic Republic, where hatred for the United States has been preached as state doctrine for twenty-two years, twenty-two football players and a hundred thousand viewers express their sympathy with the United States of America: no one could have imagined that just a weekend earlier; and, what is more, those sixty seconds of silence could one day come to be seen as a watershed in the disastrous history of American–Iranian relations.

The anti-Americanism that is widespread even among secularist intellectuals in the Middle East cannot be entirely dismissed as fanatical and irrational: a country such as Iran has often suffered under Washington's foreign policy, beginning with the CIA coup against the democratic Mosaddegh government in 1953, again with the practically colonial treatment under the shah, and with US support for Saddam Hussein's 1980 invasion, up to the destruction of a fully laden

Iranian airliner and decorations for the generals responsible near the end of the subsequent Gulf War. Except that now such sentiment is outweighed, in Iran and other countries in the region, both among elites and in the general population, by a completely opposite one, the simplest human instinct: not this. This is intolerable. The collective feeling is so strong that even the most conservative leaders don't dare counter it.

Not everyone is filled only with sympathy, to be sure, even if we discount the unfortunately exaggerated joy of some Palestinians at the 9/11 attacks, which the news networks played in an endless loop: in my own conversations and in the reports of others, the rejection of violence is frequently mixed with a cynical satisfaction that the Americans are now experiencing the same suffering they have inflicted on others. But that reaction is not limited to the Middle East. Friends and colleagues report from South America, India and China of similar responses in the street or among acquaintances, and even in public discussions in Germany's left-leaning circles the grief for the victims sometimes does not appear to run very deep.

These are well-known patterns of behaviour, obstinate and reprehensible, but not a general mood. What predominates everywhere, both here and in the Middle East, is the opposite – something less well known: terror, helplessness, sorrow at what happened to America seven days ago; moreover, the admission that perhaps criticism of American foreign policy has not been distinguished clearly enough in the past from condemnation of a whole nation.

In the Islamic countries, and among Muslims in Germany, there is an unmistakable need to repudiate the perpetrators ostentatiously, in part because the reporting on television and in the tabloids has contributed to a blanket suspicion against Islam. The fact that Palestinians donated blood for

Americans, young people in Tehran lit candles, and heavily veiled Lebanese women – including relatives of the perpetrators – gathered in public mourning in front of the American embassy in Beirut is incredible in view of the recent history of these nations and the not exactly favourable influence of the United States.

In large parts of the world, for some days at least, a basic civilizational consensus seems to be making itself felt: the consensus that murdering innocent people must not be a political instrument. The opportunities that could grow out of this new constellation, for the Middle East conflict or for relations between the West and the Islamic world, can hardly be overestimated, especially as the spontaneous emotional unanimity of the societies is reflected for once in these countries' political statements.

In the Middle East as elsewhere, rulers are guided less by emotions than by interests, so that their expressions of condolence cannot necessarily be taken as indications of true mourning; nevertheless, it is remarkable that every state in the Islamic world, with the exception of Iraq and Afghanistan, has harshly condemned the terrorist attacks in the United States. This degree of unanimity is unprecedented and opens up new, more hopeful prospects for diplomacy.

A wise Western policy would take the Islamic countries at their word and, instead of ostracizing them, would include them in the fight against terrorism. The opportunities to do so are real and have not just been discovered in the past week: they involve, first of all, isolating the terrorists and their Afghan patrons and cutting them off from their Pakistani supply lines and their Saudi financiers. This has failed in the past, not because of the other neighbouring states but because the United States has not brought enough pressure to bear on its allies Saudi Arabia and Pakistan. Such an alliance for the pacification of Afghanistan, which the United

Nations tried to establish years ago, would not be able from its inception to prevent further attacks, but it would offer a far more realistic way of drying up the most important headwater region of Islamist terror than carpet bombing.

The prerequisite for a trans-cultural collaboration against political violence would be for the West, if it decides to carry out the expected rapid military response to the terrorist attacks, to target the terror organizations specifically, not callously accepting collateral damage to the civilian population, who have already suffered maltreatment by the oppressive Taliban regime and the decades of civil war. Television footage of bombed-out Afghan villages and cities, lamenting women and murdered babies would liquidate the consensus of the civilizations before it even had a chance to take political shape. In the long term, another requirement would be to pay more attention to the legitimate interests of the populations in order to gradually defuse the legacy of anti-Americanism, especially in two regions of conflict: in the Middle East, of course, but also in the criminally neglected belt that runs from Kashmir in the south to the Central Asian republics north of Afghanistan. For years, American experts in particular have pointed to the global political danger that emanates from the many unresolved conflicts, the impoverishment and the deterioration of state structures in this atomically armed region. And, if it thought another step ahead, Washington would support not criminal and corrupt regimes in the region for the sake of its own short-term political interests but the development of civil societies – for only these can ultimately offer the stability and the minimum of social justice that would suffocate extremism.

On a smaller scale, Germany faces a comparable decision on its future course. Now more than ever, a smart domestic policy in Germany would demonstratively include the Muslims living here in the society's shared values – would include their dignitaries in public manifestations of mourning instead of repeating polarizing references to an attack on 'our' civilization, and so implicitly relegating the members of that 'other' civilization who live here to the attackers. From the point of view of security policy as well, that would be the best way to sensitize the Muslim congregations to extremist members and groups so that, in future, none are silently tolerated out of a misplaced sense of solidarity. Although the German president has sent important signals to this effect, and other leading politicians and at least the public broadcasting networks, after the initial clash-of-civilizations rhetoric, have clearly striven for a more nuanced view in the past three, four days, the domestic action of the federal government sends a different message.

Inevitable though it may be to refer to the context of the recent attacks in the continuing discussion of the projected reform of immigration law, it is delusional to believe that tightening the existing or currently planned restrictions would prevent law-abiding immigrants, even those who have actively pursued 'integration' in the sense in which the Christian Democrat leader Friedrich Merz uses the word – retaining nothing of their culture of origin except folklore – from turning out to be terrorists. The connection that the home minister Otto Schily immediately and quasi-automatically drew between the two Hamburg students identified as suspected terrorists and the country's whole immigration policy pre-emptively panders to those minds that just as automatically see a potential extremist in every Eastern-looking neighbour.

Equating the attackers with the culture they come from has already poisoned the atmosphere in Germany. Probably most Muslims in Germany have experienced insults, harassment or death threats either personally or among their friends and acquaintances. The comments now circulating on the internet are often too offensive to quote and are a mirror image of what can be observed in certain Arabic chat rooms: the clash of civilizations that criminals such as Osama bin Laden have wanted to bomb into being for years is now being waged online. Booksellers tell of numerous requests for Huntington's intellectually lazy work, which contains – regardless of its conclusions, which one may reject or accept – numerous errors and incorrect information.

There exists a danger that Huntington's thesis of the clash of civilizations could gain political and military influence at the very moment when, for the first time, under the impression of the pictures from New York and Washington, a worldwide civilizational consensus on the condemnation of terrorism could materialize. Then the attackers would have achieved the goal for which they took thousands of people with them to their deaths.

4

THE SOFT WORDS
OF VIOLENCE

After the Beginning of the War in Afghanistan
Süddeutsche Zeitung, 11 October 2001

Osama bin Laden speaks beautiful Arabic. No dialect expressions creep into his speech, as they do with other members of the present generation of leaders in the Arab world, nor does he confuse the complicated grammatical inflections, as even intellectuals sometimes do. He chooses old-fashioned words, which are familiar to educated Arabs from religious literature and from classical poetry, and he carefully avoids all neologisms. His articulation of the astoundingly nuanced Standard Arabic consonants and the modulation and length of his vowels could be more precise – this betrays his lack of theological training, which teaches Arabic elocution along with Quran recitation. But, at the same time, it is precisely his painstakingly modest diction that seeks to move the hearts of his brothers in faith. While his garb and the setting of the video are intended to generate a prophetic aura, his verbal asceticism is a reminder of the military and political inferiority of the early Muslims, which they made up for many times over by the purity of their faith. Even the lack of intonation in bin Laden's rhetoric proclaims the puritanical Wahhabi temperament, which is allegedly identical with that of God's messenger.

A similar abstinence from aesthetic splendour is known in Protestantism, while the Muslim tradition, building on the verbal intensity of the Quran, has always emphasized and taught the magnificence of words. The heirs of this tradition include the great Arabic poets of the present day, many of them poets of freedom, such as Adonis and Mahmoud Darwish, who recite their verses dramatically, as works of acoustic art; but its heirs also include the political and religious leaders of the contemporary Arab world who seek to drown the banality of their statements in magniloquence and pathos. It is from them especially that the man in the mountains is distinguishing himself by relying on a clear calmness of expression.

The break with the dominant tradition is most obvious when Osama bin Laden quotes phrases from the Quran: where other speakers grotesquely tend to raise and lower their voices as soon as they pronounce the revelation, bin Laden goes on in the same fastidious tone, as if he wanted to persuade his listeners through the logic of his message alone. Who knows to what degree he realizes himself that the abstinence from all rhetoric, in this situation, when the Western world is stylizing him as the epitome of evil, is the cleverest rhetorical device? Be that as it may, Osama bin Laden has achieved with a seven-minute speech at least as great a media coup in the Muslim world as George W. Bush did in the United States with his transformation, within days, from an insecure, verbally unpredictable cowboy into a resolute world statesman.

The inequality of their military means – on this side, a few box cutters to humiliate a superpower; on the other, the most powerful weaponry in the world to bombard one of the world's poorest countries – is matched by the difference in their propagandistic equipment: on this side, a video camera; on that, an army of advisors, television networks and agencies. Yet each adversary is addressing only his own public, Islamic or Western, even where they are formally speaking to that of the opponent. Osama bin Laden's threats to the Americans are intended to put him forward as a standard-bearer for those who feel themselves threatened by America.

George W. Bush's new tireless praise of Islam can only reach the ears of potentially wavering allies in Europe, and possibly the Muslims in America. In the light of America's foreign policy in the Middle East, his friendly words sound just as cynical in the Islamic world itself as the food packages that his army drops alongside bombs over Afghanistan. If the American government was interested in winning over public opinion in the Islamic countries, it would have obtained a stronger mandate from the United Nations, presented evidence for its accusations in a verifiable way, and actually taken strategic aim at terrorism instead of beginning yet another long-term military deployment in Central Asia and using weapons – such as B-52 bombers – which are obviously not suitable for smoking out specific hide-outs.

Up until his speech, Osama bin Laden was more a phantom than a real figure to the Islamic world. Of course, his biographies are circulated in some countries, but most people know him from the few interview clips that have been repeated on CNN, the BBC and Al Jazeera. Before the CIA declared him the head terrorist a few years ago (which was shortly after the last time they had provided an escort for him), he was practically unknown. He has not published any books, developed any doctrine, or even allowed his speeches to be recorded – he was the enemy of the United States, and that was enough for the extremists to accept him as their fatherly friend. For the head of maybe three, maybe five thousand extremists to be declared the chief enemy of the entire Western world at all, for him to appear in the media as the counterpart to the American president and not as the criminal and murderer that he is, surpasses the wildest hopes of even the most intelligent terrorist.

But now this phantom suddenly speaks to the people in the Islamic world and does not appear at all like the demon he has been made out to be. Although his words express a fanatical will to fight, he speaks not fanatically, but softly, cautiously, in a simple, persuasive Arabic. And much of what he says corresponds in the Muslim world to what many people, peaceful people, think, but few politicians dare to say this simply: about the suffering of the Palestinians, the role of American foreign policy, the double standards and the feeling of being oppressed and humiliated by the West day in and day out. As one-sided as that picture is, it is no more so than the picture of the Islamic world painted here by talk shows, best-sellers and unspeakable documentaries.

To win the hitherto peaceful majority of Muslims over to his side, Osama bin Laden had to wait until last Sunday to publish his first video. As long as the United States had not bombed Afghanistan, there would have been no chance of appealing to broad segments of the population, since there was no chance of shaking off the role of the aggressor. Like everyone who wages war, he first had to cast himself as the victim to legitimize his own attacks – and with them the deaths of innocent people. For that reason, although by a pure logic of terrorism he could have boasted of them, he did not take responsibility for the attacks in New York and Washington but only hailed them as a just punishment.

But now, after the retaliatory bombings that he certainly expected, if not craved, he can present his combat as defensive without exposing himself to ridicule from all sides. He can call the Americans terrorists and invoke the bombed

Afghan nation as witnesses against the United States in an appeal for solidarity among his brothers in faith. It does not take Bush's use of the word 'crusade' or Berlusconi's announcement that the Islamic world will be conquered to show that the argument's mechanism is not so unknown in the West. When the American president, in his most recent address, praises a fourth-grader's willingness 'to give' him her dad, that is almost identical with statements from Muslim 'martyr families'. And the language in which Bush speaks to the Americans, by the way, the already broad English of the South which he speaks with marked slowness and celebrates with as many pauses as only a Western hero can, suggests gritty authenticity just as much as the Arabic of his arch-enemy – and is just as artificial: those who search for old recordings of George W. Bush will be surprised to hear a very common American English and an ordinary intonation, without an overly obvious Texas accent.

Osama bin Laden will not persuade the majority of Muslims. Most people in the Islamic world can see through his simple ploy, and none other than the president of an Islamic Republic, Mohammad Khatami, has called it out in gratifying clarity. Osama bin Laden is a suspected mass murderer; his interpretation of Islam contradicts all the accepted doctrines. But, after this speech, those who tend to believe him are, as far as telephone conversations and commentaries permit a conjecture, no longer just scattered radicals but broader segments of society, at least in the Arab world, Indonesia and Pakistan. In these countries, public opinion is not reversing, but it is threatening to shift significantly to the terrorists' advantage.

Before the speech, too, it was not certain that most Arabs or Pakistanis would follow their leaders in unreservedly taking the side of the United States, but it seemed far less certain that the terrorists' plan – that of instigating an uprising of

Muslims against their own leaders – would succeed. Since last Sunday, the specific danger is that a politically significant minority in the Islamic world is inclined to draw a disastrous conclusion from Bush's Manichaean rhetoric and his precept that there is 'no neutrality' in this struggle: the conclusion that he is right. That is the conclusion that Osama bin Laden proposes when he says the whole world is now divided into two camps, the faithful and the unbelievers.

5

WHAT ALTERNATIVE?

Before the War in Iraq

Süddeutsche Zeitung, 27 February 2003

The United States has managed to persuade almost no one in the world that its interest in a war against Iraq has to do with weapons of mass destruction. To deflect the propagandistic fiasco, it has come up with a second argument: democracy, which is to be established in Baghdad and in the entire Middle East. If we subtract the idealism of this argument, it is not so very far removed from what Washington is actually doing: violent regime change as part of a hegemonic order in a region which is seen as important for the United States' own security, economy and energy supply.

The fact that the first argument was so much easier to rebut than all the reasons for all the wars of past decades is what allowed the peace movement to grow so strong. It is ridiculous to claim that a demoralized and militarily destitute country such as Iraq, where every square foot has been surveilled for years by satellite cameras and reconnaissance aircraft, represents an acute danger to world peace, much less one comparable with Nazi Germany. But the peace movement has not yet thought of an answer to the second argument. That is its great weakness, because at the moment Saddam Hussein is reinterpreting the 'no' to war as a 'yes' to his dictatorship. As contrived as the current US government's engagement for human rights may be, hypocrisy in Washington does not make the regime in Baghdad more tolerable. A Pax Americana is no longer a great promise today – but wouldn't it be a better prospect for the people in Iraq than the thoroughly bleak status quo? Those who would credibly oppose war should ask themselves this question instead of just reciting the litany about oil. Only the pacifists and the supporters of the American president will find an unequivocal answer; everyone else will be unable to avoid that most unpleasant exertion of the intellect: weighing the pros and cons. Although it sounds almost heretical in these days, there are reasons in favour of a war. You don't have to believe Donald Rumsfeld to take them seriously; you only have to ask around among Iraqi Shiites, Kurds and exiles.

Nonetheless, this author, while acknowledging the opportunities that a regime change would bring, tends to consider the dangers of a war against Iraq unacceptable. Even if we discount all the unpredictable consequences – the numbers of civilian casualties and the degree of destruction; the proverbial scorched earth that Saddam might leave behind; the possibility of a second Afghanistan in Iraq; the threat of instability in the rest of the Middle East; the Israeli thought experiments about what could be done with the Palestinians in the wake of the American invasion; and much more – even discounting all of these unknowns, one thing is clear: terrorism can be expected to grow substantially as a result of an invasion, whether because the existing groups will be motivated to commit new attacks or because new groups could form anywhere, even with no more than conceptual ties to Al Qaeda. The counter-measures that can be expected will motivate still further attacks, and thus the spiral of violence that is already racking Israel and Palestine would finally become global.

Expressing such misgivings may seem like yielding to terror without a fight but, in fact, the logic of terrorism has the opposite aim: namely, to deter those attacked from political action and provoke them to violence. The fight against terror in Europe will undermine fundamental values of our own civilization – a process we can already observe in the United States – and in that way advance the terrorists' goals. And even if none of the dangers mentioned should materialize, and Saddam Hussein is sitting in a plane to The Hague two days after the war begins, an easy victory over Iraq would invigorate the Bush administration's imperialism in messianic clothing, making it scarier than ever. These are a few briefly stated reasons against the war, assuming an American puppet regime in Baghdad is preferable to Saddam Hussein. But they are not enough. Being against the war does not answer the question of what the future of Iraq would look like without a war.

The Europeans accuse the Americans of being unable to show any realistic plans for the post-war scenario, but they themselves have no plans, however unrealistic, for the no-war scenario. Are things just supposed to go on as they have for the past twelve years? The demonstrators all over the world may proclaim they're not *against* something, but *for* peace – do they mean a peace in which Saddam Hussein's regime and a murderous embargo persist? Must hundreds of thousands of children continue to die in such a peace (as they have since the beginning of the embargo)? Must a rich, industrialized country such as Iraq be thrown back economically into the eighteenth century? Is that supposed to be the alternative to war?

The opponents of war should not limit themselves to saying 'no'; they should also think about medium-term prospects for Iraq to shake off the embargo and the tyranny. Are there no solutions at hand? Correct – and that means we should have started looking for them long ago. The country's present situation is so bad for the population that even Europe's diplomacy should have been able to develop plans to improve it. That wouldn't have to mean an OSCE for the Middle East with hopes of resolving the conflict between Palestinians and Israelis in the same fell swoop. Of course an overall plan would improve the chances of change in Iraq as well, but under the existing constellation – with Sharon replacing Rabin, Bush Jr. replacing Clinton, and an Arafat who would govern the ruins of his office building, if anything – it would be absolutely unrealistic.

The American war plans are only the last link in a chain of fatal mistakes and avoidable crises in Western policy towards Iraq. The chain runs from support for Saddam Hussein in the war of aggression against Iran to President Bush Senior's decision not to end the second Gulf War with the regime change that would have been comparatively easy then, and to the disastrous sanctions policy. But now the situation is what it is: the country is devastated, Saddam Hussein holds his people hostage, and the American troops are on Iraq's borders. Instead of moaning over mistakes and missed opportunities, it is more important even now to formulate alternatives to war. With the tremendous international pressure weighing on Saddam Hussein, more is possible than just forcing him to give up the last 2 per cent of his former military strength.

Saddam Hussein is not Osama bin Laden. His interest is not in ideology or religion but in power and personal advantage. He has repeatedly demonstrated his political adaptability and the cool rationality of his actions. A prospect of his personal survival and the end of sanctions could be used to involve Saddam Hussein in a political process which would contain him within his own borders while restraining him domestically and undermining the foundations of his power in the medium term. There are many examples – from Iran to Indonesia, from South Korea to South Africa or, in Europe, Spain and Portugal – which show that reforms introduced in a repressive state in response to external pressure can also develop a momentum of their own as information flows into the country or structures of civil society form. A prerequisite for such a development in the case of Iraq would be a more specific embargo, or 'smart sanctions', precisely targeting the privileges and assets of the ruling clique instead of smiting, as now, the whole population and especially the secular middle class, who are essential for a peaceful transformation. The instruments of Western diplomacy, those it once developed through détente, are not spectacular and do not guarantee success. But all experience shows that they offer the only realistic way to deal with a dictatorship when military action is too risky.

War is the wrong means. But liberation is not the wrong end.

6

RIGHT AGAIN, SADLY

The Attack on the Synagogue in Istanbul

Süddeutsche Zeitung, 27 November 2003

Experts are sometimes right. Those who did not depend on Fox News or RTL 2 alone for their information may have known that the United States would quickly win a war against Saddam Hussein's Iraq. The much greater challenge – as we were informed in the major European newspapers, but also in the critical Arabic and American press – the greater challenge lay in establishing a stable post-war order. Of course there were the notorious Islam experts, with their litanies about religious masses throwing themselves in the path of the American tanks and predictions of an immediate conflagration of the entire region, just like their earlier warnings about the suicidal Afghan warrior race. However, most academics, the serious journalists and even most of the conservatives among Europe's foreign policy leaders anticipated that the Americans' success or failure in Iraq would become apparent only in the months and years following the overthrow of Saddam.

Before the Iraq war, we read that the Iraqis would be glad to see the end of the dictatorship, but not necessarily hail the Americans as liberators. We read that Iraq, for all its domestic brutality, was much too weak militarily to pose a threat to world peace. Consequently, no one is seriously surprised that the search for weapons of mass destruction in Iraq was unsuccessful. Anyone watching the evening news could have predicted that the second reason for war – Saddam's links with international terrorism – would also prove obsolete. The United States could not possibly have been counting on the sympathy of the Iraqi population when it placed the reconstruction of Iraq in the hands of certain American companies, some of which are also closely connected with members of the Bush government. And, as if Washington wanted to live up to every last cliché of anti-Americanism, it allowed missionaries of Franklin Graham's evangelical–fundamentalist organization 'Samaritan's Purse' to swarm out all over Iraq immediately after the fall of Baghdad. In the West, Graham's father Billy may be remembered for having led the current president of the US to faith after his withdrawal from alcohol and for speaking the invocation at his inauguration. In the Muslim world, on the other hand, it is also remembered that Graham pronounced Islam 'a very evil and wicked religion' shortly before the Iraq War.

The warnings could not have been more precise: the predictable instability in Iraq would shake the whole region; a war against Iraq in violation of international law would not only stoke anti-Western sentiment and create a thousand new bin Ladens, as the Egyptian president Mubarak had prophesied, but would quite specifically give bin Laden's fighters a new refuge, after Afghanistan and those parts of Pakistan which had become uncontrollable, which would offer them much more advantageous strategic conditions; an anti-terror campaign waged in such a blind rage would lead to further acts of terror, which would ultimately reach Europe as well. George W. Bush's recent pronouncement that Iraq has become a centre of international terrorism is not incorrect, and it would be a fatal mistake for America to leave this country to its fate now that it has become ungoverned and consequently ravaged by Islamists of all countries. At the same time, however, Bush's pronouncement is an admission that America, by launching its war, created the necessity of its presence in Iraq in the first place.

Since the terrorist attack on the synagogue in Istanbul, one last and particularly frightening criticism of American foreign policy has finally proved realistic: the warning against a new Muslim anti-Judaism fed by the perception that Washington does nothing in the Middle East except enforce Israeli interests. No one could have seriously believed Bush's promise that the liberation of Iraq would bring the conflict between Israelis and Palestinians closer to resolution because Saddam's alleged financing of the suicide bombers would cease. On the contrary, there were many and varied predictions that the United States' unprecedented alignment with the most radical government in the history of Israel would further inflame an anti-Jewish animosity that had already grown frightening enough. In view of a political position that identifies Israel's government with the interests of Jews, it is reprehensible and despicable, but not surprising, when criticism of Israel turns into enmity against Jews. The assurances of many Muslims notwithstanding, this sentiment has become unmistakable. It has become a menace to Jews all over the world and, at the same time, an opium to many Muslims who would rather make accusations against other nations than look among themselves for the reasons for backwardness and deficits in democracy.

The fact that Judeophobia in the Muslim world has no historic roots comparable with those of European anti-Semitism does not make it harmless or less heinous. The effects it could have on the situation in the Middle East, and also on the coexistence of Muslims and Jews in the West, hardly bear thinking about. This anti-Jewish sentiment must be fought nowhere else but in the Muslim public sphere. That means, first of all, finally acknowledging the antagonism which has cost the lives of innocent Jews in Israel, on Djerba, and elsewhere in the world, instead of continually asserting that it is resistance directed only against the state of Israel.

As shamefully quiet as the self-critical voices have been to date, they will not grow louder if the American Middle East policy defends those actions committed by Israel that it rightly combats when they are committed by Muslim states: oppression and violence against civilians. It is hard to top the cynicism of Sharon's pronouncement that Europe, by its criticism of Israel's policy, is guilty of the Istanbul attacks. He might better have addressed Wolfowitz and Cheney, who in the past equated peace in the Occupied Territories with breaking the resistance of the Palestinians.

No well-informed person can claim today that they were not made aware of this scenario. And yet it took place, with eerie precision. That raises the question why the United States, against all available knowledge, carries out precisely that policy that practically calls forth rejection and new attacks. Ultimately, the engagement in Iraq doesn't even serve the interests of the American economy (except for a few companies and industries), as the anti-imperialist reflex would assume. This cannot be attributed to stupidity, nor to the government in Washington being worse informed than the rest of the world. Did that government then consciously take the risk, after 11 September – or, to be more exact, after the largely accepted war against the Taliban – that most of its allies, with the exception of Israel, would today be perturbed by its foreign policy?

Whether the escalation in the Middle East is the result of mistaken assessments or part of a strategy of using each new threat as a legitimation of force and thus cementing

American dominance, the fact remains: after 9/11, considerable strands of Western foreign policy elude ordinary rational realpolitical understanding, which is concerned with – besides stability – national advantage, national security and national reputation. Thus the war on terror is dominated by calculated irrationality on both sides.

On the one side we are dealing with extremists who care nothing for public opinion in the Muslim countries, and hence for realpolitical goals – otherwise they wouldn't blow people up indiscriminately, including Muslims. No dialogue is possible with them, nor are they receptive to appeals in the name of Islam or humanity – they can only be fought by every means tolerable under the rule of law. On the other side, we are dealing with a policy in Washington and Jerusalem which, as far as we can discern, does exactly what advances terrorism. That does not mean that the two sides are equal or even equally morally reprehensible. In addition to all the other differences, one is particularly important: on this side of the front, we are dealing with democratically elected governments. That is the main reason why some hope remains that at least the experts' worst predictions will not come true.

A different government in Washington might follow the example of the British in southern Iraq, who, instead of emphasizing military occupation, are effectively supporting civil processes and suggesting that democracy is possible in an Arab country. A different American government would not remain apathetically acquiescent towards Putin's genocide in Chechnya and towards the criminal regimes in Central Asia denouncing and suppressing every democratic protest as Islamist. It would offer far more resolute support to Afghanistan's government, which so far is little more than a municipal administration of Kabul. But, most of all, a different government in Washington would seize the chance offered by the fatigue of Israelis and Palestinians, a chance that has finally been given a realistic expression in the Geneva Initiative. Israeli opposition leaders and Palestinian intimates of Arafat have formulated concrete proposals to solve the problems in the interrupted peace process. According to a survey by the Israeli daily *Haaretz*, the initiative, which is supposed to be signed in December, is supported by a majority of both nations. Instead of acquiescing in Sharon's defamation of the Israeli negotiators as traitors, a wise foreign policy which believes in the security and continued existence of Israel would support such negotiators as well as their Palestinian counterparts. None of these measures would quickly stop the Islamist terror – it has already become much too self-reinforcing. But together they could prevent the thousand bin Ladens that exist now from becoming a million tomorrow.

7

Strategy of Escalation

On the Hostages in Beslan

Neue Zürcher Zeitung, 11 September 2004

The only thing that is still surprising about the Muslim extremists' acts of terrorism is that the perpetrators are still able to escalate their terror from one to the next. Did it not seem as though the last remaining scruple of modern civilization – that is, not wanting to see nor to show the act of killing – had been blatantly abandoned when Iraqi kidnappers beheaded the American Nick Berg on camera? There are still more scruples left, the world realizes with horror, and they can be thrown away still more flagrantly: by the intentional sacrifice of more than a hundred children. It is probably part of the logic of contemporary terrorism to surpass itself: only in this way can the perpetrators break the power of habituation with every successive act and so prevent the international media from relegating them to the back pages in its news. Not only are we loth to imagine what will happen next to keep the special-feature broadcasts going worldwide, but we can hardly imagine that the brutality has long since reached a degree that the sheltered post-war generations of the West had thought impossible outside the world of fiction. It is a brutality known up to now only from horror films and snuff videos. To the hostage-takers of Beslan too, no doubt.

Terror struggles against its own ritualization, almost desperately it seems, yet, as it breaks successive taboos, its very escalation seems to become a ritual. Everything else remains the same: the images, no matter where and against whom an attack is committed, of paramedics and barricades, ambulances rushing away and relatives left behind, politicians displaying empathy at bedsides and martial resolution in press conferences. The sentences in which government representatives react to the murder of their citizens – in Israel, in the United States, recently in Iraq, now in Russia again – are identical, word for word.

By disregarding all regional differences and intoning the knee-jerk soundbite about combating international terrorism even more mercilessly, they do the perpetrators of one act after another the favour of raising them to their eye level, stylizing them as enemies in a third world war which has long since begun. But – what is worse – in the war on terrorism, the face of our own civilization threatens to become so ugly that it could soon resemble the grotesque portrait which the terrorists paint of their enemy. You can't comprehend how it is when the body parts fly past you, say even well-meaning intellectuals in countries on the front lines of terrorism when they are admonished by outsiders to be cautious and politically rational. We will make you understand how it is when your own children are murdered, cried a terrorist in Beslan to a hostage who asked why, of all places, they had stormed a school.

From summit meeting to summit meeting, from attack to attack, ever farther-reaching counter-measures are adopted to fight international terrorism. Here, too, the taboos fall like ripe fruits: while Europe has limited itself up to now to new laws, Islamophobic clashes of civilizations and crude best-sellers, the remedies elsewhere are torture, expulsion and open lawlessness. But when the members of the coalition against international terrorism react to each attack with ever more draconian laws and world war rhetoric, threats and exclusion, they begin in their turn to approach a mirror image of the terrorists' broken taboos.

Those who question the dialectics of escalation and point to the root causes of the violence are declared accomplices of terror; those who speak of political negotiations or even peaceful solutions are pronounced poor naive fools. 'Beware the Understanding Trap!' the weekly *Die Zeit* warns its readers on page 1. There's no negotiating with terrorists, the saying goes; terrorism understands no language but severity. Could it not be that precisely this is the mistake in the fight against terror: speaking the language that the terrorists understand? By doing so, the coalition members may be entering into a communication with the terrorists that practically challenges them to respond again. In any case, it is time for an evaluation of the results so far in the war on terror before there are still more civilian casualties to be mourned and still more terrorists to be fought.

It is difficult to object to the expansion of police and intelligence activities that appear to be specifically aimed at detecting possible attackers. Every foiled act of violence renews the legitimacy of state intervention up to the limits of what is compatible with the rule of law. But individual successes in combating terror will be for nought as long as governments are fooled into speaking the language of terrorists. The fight against terror will only be crowned with lasting success if it returns to what terrorists do not master: politics. Certainly, people who are already resolved to commit mass murder cannot be elevated to political partners. But we can try to prevent every terrorist caught or killed from attracting hundreds of new recruits.

There is no example in recent time of a long-term victory over terrorism merely by ever more ruthless counter-measures – not in Israel, not in Chechnya, not in Iraq or Kashmir. On the contrary, the numbers and dimensions of the acts of violence have always been much smaller when a political solution at least did not seem to be impossible: during the peace process in the Middle East, during the shuttle diplomacy of Indians and Pakistanis over Kashmir, since the Israeli withdrawal from Lebanon, between Russia's two Chechen wars – or, to name two more of many less prominent examples, in the Indonesian province of Aceh and in the Tajik civil war. We do not have to negotiate with terrorists. But we shouldn't keep negotiations on hold as long as there are terrorists. Most of all, though, we should not do everything possible, as the Russian government does, to make potential negotiating partners eventually become terrorists.

Just recently, the Shiite grand ayatollah Sistani showed the heavily armed Americans and the amazed world how to pacify an embattled city such as Najaf without fighting. The example may be too special to be applicable to other battlegrounds of terror. But the principle that al-Sistani introduced in the conflict between de facto occupiers and so-called resistance groups is realpolitically more successful than war on terror. It is the principle of upholding the primacy of politics even when the opponents violate it. The war on terror up to now has failed so grotesquely that waging peace would be worth a try. Nothing could surprise the terrorists more.

8

A GOOD THING YOU'RE EDUCATING ME...

Confusion in the Integration Debate

die tageszeitung, 20 November 2004

I have noticed that most people who get worked up about the foreigners, or, to be more exact, about the Turks – no, that's not it either; after all, the telly these days is always showing perfectly good Turks, who have given up wearing headscarves and begun complaining about the Turks – let me say it this way: most people who get worked up about fundamentalism ... fundamentalism, fundamentalism, that's good; Muslim fundamentalism to be exact, Islamism I mean – that's what I'll say, although Islam is fundamentalist anyway, at least if you believe in it; Islam is misogynistic and glorifies violence, there's that surah about women standing below men, and about how you're supposed to kill the unbelievers, kill us all – kill *you* all, I mean, me being one of the murderers – of course there are plenty of verses like that in the Bible but, my God, we've had the Enlightenment, whereas the Muslims are still living in the Middle Ages, and, besides, our religion is the religion of love – *your* religion I mean, me still living in the Middle Ages with my religion of violence – and if I'm not beating my wife and not forcing my daughter to marry and not committing a suicide bombing, it's because you've educated me in the spirit of tolerance and Enlightenment, purified me of my fundamentalist tradition; I can hardly have learned it from my parents, they're Islamofascists, whereas you: my God, how you love everybody, especially the poor persecuted Turkish women whom you don't give housing and jobs to because they're persecuted, not by you that is, but persecuted by the Muslims, by their Muslim Islamofascist husbands, and so you have to spit on them in the street so they know how persecuted they are, and God forbid we should let the poor persecuted Islamofascist brainwashed headscarfed women loose on schoolchildren, for love's sake I mean, for love of the children, and also of course for love of the poor Muslim women who've been forced under the burka; you really are a culture of tolerance and brotherly love, only now do I really realize it, I'm so sorry, dear tabloid press, dear newsweeklies, dear second-wave feminists, that it's taken me until now to realize it, how you loved the Jews especially, and the Blacks; and domestic violence – is something you don't have, of course, utterly unknown, and if there is violence in families, which there isn't, it obviously has nothing, absolutely nothing to do with your culture, much less your religion, and what's more the asylum seekers, my word, how you loved them when you set them on fire in Rostock, you tolerant Germans with your brotherly love; okay, that was a bit strong perhaps, better to love the asylum seekers at night in the side streets when no one's looking, besides, you have to see it in proportion, no one ever talks about that, there were barely a hundred foreigners killed in the nineties, that's nothing to the thousands brutally murdered on 9/11 by these Islamofascists who took advantage of our tolerance, our tolerance and brotherly love, they got too much love, these Muslims, too much tolerance, and then in Madrid and on Djerba, that's the dimensions of the problem, they want to kill us all – *you* all, I mean – at least I've noticed that most people who get worked up about Islamofascism never met a Muslim except maybe on holiday or in a restaurant, because they live either in the Eastern states, where Muslims hardly dare go to begin with, or in neighbourhoods where there are only good foreigners, moderate foreigners as the lovely expression has it – I'm sorry, moderate Muslims I mean, although of course that's a contradiction in terms, but you can hardly say non-Muslim Muslims, or ex-Muslims, the way you say ex-Nazi or ex-wife, but never mind, I just wanted to say there are good Muslims too, as you can read everywhere in the press, divorced Muslims so to speak, Muslims who are divorced from Islam and their fascist parents, who send their children to the Montessori school and bring lovely sweets to parents' evening, lovely little Islamofascist sweets, but soaked in the spirit of Christian love and Western tolerance so they really integrate in our – no, your – secular society and in the Montessori school, and that's what we want of course – I mean, what *you* want; integration is incredibly good, so no one can say we have anything against Islam – *you* have anything against Islam, I mean – against me, that is; I always forget I'm one of the evil people; I don't feel so evil but, my God, I haven't had the Enlightenment so of course I don't know how evil I am, but it's a good thing you're educating me, otherwise I'd be committing a suicide bombing at parents' evening and a forced marriage with the teacher first.

9

DESPERATION AND ENTHUSIASM

After the French Referendum on the European Constitution

Süddeutsche Zeitung, 3 June 2005

To those French citizens who lost the referendum on the European constitution on Sunday, Europe is just as much a political project as it is to the political and cultural elites in Germany, Spain, Great Britain and the Netherlands. They are striving to unite Europe, but their personal and political livelihood does not depend on that project. If necessary, they can live without Europe: as Germans, as Spaniards, as Dutch, as British. I believe it is this comparatively comfortable starting position that is to blame for the low enthusiasm that European unity evokes, both among Europe's politicians and among its citizens. There is not the desperation that attended the birth of the French–German reconciliation, for example. My situation is different. To me, Europe is a promise and a necessity. I cannot live without Europe.

My parents came to Germany from Iran over fifty years ago to study. They are very well integrated, they strive for tolerance and understanding, they are socially involved, they speak German well – they are devout Muslims in the European image. They are glad to live in Germany. They are grateful for it. But, even after fifty years, they would not describe themselves as Germans. I don't think that is entirely their fault. It may be Germany's as well.

Even I rarely hear or read that I am a German. I was born here; I have had German citizenship for several years now, in addition to Iranian; German is the language I live in and make my living from. And yet, the sentence *Sie sind Deutscher*, 'You are a German', is apparently difficult for my fellow Germans to pronounce. At most they say it in hyphenated form, almost apologetically: a German-Iranian. My cousin who has lived in the United States for six years is already unquestioningly taken for an American. But a German is not something you can become. As an immigrant, even in the second, third generation, you remain an Iranian, a Turk, an Arab. But – you can become a European. You can pledge yourself to Europe because it is an intentional community, not the name of a religion or an ethnicity. Europe is not a country. Its borders cannot be drawn in the same way the borders of a country can. Europe is an idea. I need this Europe because – where else could I go?

Readers may find it odd perhaps, but for people like me this is a serious question, an existential question. What happens if Europe doesn't want us? There is nothing theoretical about it when politicians who, according to the current polls, will be governing Germany after the parliamentary elections travel all over the country proclaiming or insinuating that Islam doesn't belong to Europe. How else can I understand them but as saying I don't belong to Europe? Should I hope for forbearance? Follow the current fashion and publish invective against my own culture in order to qualify for Europe? Or just clear out? When a politician of the rank and reputation of a Helmut Schmidt says it was a mistake to recruit migrant workers of another religion – how can I understand it except as him saying it was a mistake to recruit my parents? It is a mistake that we are here. I think seriously about where we could go, where my children could grow old, if not in a Europe that fulfils its promise as a place where people of different backgrounds, religions, languages, cultures and sexual orientations can live in equality on the basis of a secular constitution. At present, I don't know any other place where I would want to live.

The defensive attitude that is increasingly taken in talking about Europe is directed not only, and not essentially, against Muslims. It is directed against everyone who no longer belongs, or does not yet belong, to the European 'we': this includes those Eastern European countries which have been denied all prospects of joining. As this 'we' loses its openness, it loses an essential characteristic: the fundamental European values are not bound to any given background or religion; they are transferable – and, what is more, the special thing about them is that, unlike the values of a religious community or the old European nation-states, they can be shared by people of different heritages, countries and cultures. Those who take these values seriously do not exclude others from them but work to spread them. The existing European institutions lack transparency and political legitimacy? Right: then we must fight to make them democratic and constitutionally enshrined, not to weaken them. Turkey doesn't fulfil the Copenhagen criteria, which have rightly been made a condition for admission to the European Union? Right again: then Europe should do everything to ensure that Turkey changes to meet those criteria – and be proud some day if Turkey has become European.

But now, not just in Germany but throughout Western Europe, politicians are gaining popularity who speak of fears instead of opportunities, who cleave to national authorities and define criteria for exclusion instead of working for change in the countries that do not yet meet the European standards. Instead of delighting in Ms Merkel's discovery of the smile, we should pay attention to the words with which she commented on the referendum in France: here someone is trying to win elections by raising doubts instead of responding to them. As chancellor, the woman who went to Washington at the high point of the European debate on Iraq to offer her services to George W. Bush's America will not suddenly stand for a more self-assured Europe and an outwardly and inwardly strong European Union.

Whatever one may think of Schröder, Fischer and Eichel – they did not pay lip service to Europe. Of tomorrow's possible ministers – Bosbach, Stoiber, Kauder – none has yet attracted notice as a champion of European unity. We need only compare them with their predecessors in their own parties – Kohl, Schäuble, Rühe – to realize how the tide has turned. No initiative can be expected of a future government under the leadership of the Christian Democrats to overcome the madness of the twentieth century, the ideology of states based on the unity of nation, race and religion. Nor do the young neo-conservative intellectuals rallying in the better right-wing press uphold the cause of Europe – unlike the post-war elites up to and including the '68 generation.

I mentioned desperation and enthusiasm: it will come as no surprise that my desperation has grown significantly in view of the coming change of government in Germany and the French 'No' to the constitution, which will be followed by rejection in other countries and the election of still more Eurosceptics. I hope now all the more for enthusiastic Europeans.

10

HATE PICTURES
AND HYSTERIA

The Dispute over the Muhammad Cartoons
Süddeutsche Zeitung, 8 February 2006

The dispute over the caricatures in a Danish newspaper is evolving as if a screenplay author had written the script of a global clash of civilizations. The Muslims' reactions in this scenario are like those of Pavlov's dog: predictable, thoughtless, brutal. They bark when a light goes on and bite on command. A considerable part of the Iranian and Arab public has not realized that you don't resort to violence just because you feel angry or insulted; that in the globalized world there are peaceful and at the same time much more effective means of advocating your own position.

Every consumer can boycott a commodity – that is the rule of the free market economy, and American media corporations in particular would not dare risk the economic consequences of offending important customer groups. If the Muslims had followed that strategy, they could have won the current conflict and, at the same time, held up to ridicule the unprincipled Danish prime minister, who was willing to put aside his contempt for Muslims and whine, 'Please, dialogue, please!' at the first unbought feta cheese. The Muslims could have done that and, for all the indignation they would have inspired in Europe, they would have been sure of the sympathy of a large proportion of global public opinion – including many American correspondents rubbing their eyes at the spreading racism in European media. But once again it has transpired that many Muslims want to live in the modern world but fail to understand or to accept its rules.

You can boycott products, write articles, waste money on media campaigns, lobby politicians – but no one has the right to burn flags, much less storm embassies. Many things about the rioters' behaviour can be explained (such as their instrumentalization by dictatorial regimes), but nothing can be excused. They have dragged their Prophet's legacy and Islam's prestige through far more mud than Europe's right-wing extremists could have imagined in their most cynical dreams. The Muslim mob shows how far removed the Arab public spheres still are from the standards of civility, the fairness and the even-handedness that they expect from the West.

On the other side of the clash of cultures, there was at first a Danish newspaper on the political right margin of a country which as a whole has slid far to the right in recent years and enacted laws that openly contradict the achievements and values of European civilization. For four months, that newspaper had not managed to seriously provoke the Muslim community in Denmark; it sent out the tasteless cartoons again and again until it finally found a few zealots who took the desired offence. The provocation does not excuse the reaction of some imams in Denmark and of parts of the Iranian and Arab public sphere. But if you wave a red rag long enough, eventually even the most lethargic bull will start to move. And, sadly, many Arabs and Muslims are behaving like bulls of very limited intelligence and comprehension when they go wild over a few badly drawn caricatures.

Anyone who knows even a little about Middle Eastern literature knows that it is crawling with fools who drag everything through the mud, and I mean everything, including God, the clergy, and naturally the rulers (although in fact the prophets – all prophets – have been mostly exempted). The prohibition against portraying Muhammad has of course been violated again and again in the course of history; Islamic culture itself for that matter could be described, especially in its medieval heyday, as a continual violation of its own taboos. And the most acerbic jokes about Islam can be heard in Tehran, Beirut or Istanbul, where they are sometimes appreciatively repeated by mischievous mullahs. In Iran, the jokes that are told only among racists are those about the Jewish and Christian minorities. No one who is interested in a peaceful coexistence of the religions in Iran would laugh at them.

But it is also true, as an Iranian newspaper's call for submissions of anti-Semitic caricatures demonstrates, that the current Iranian president, Mahmoud Ahmadinejad, and the coalition government he leads are not interested in such a peaceful balance. Should we follow his example? The Europeans could not do him a greater favour than to throw their own standards and ideals overboard. Unfortunately, many intellectuals, journalists and politicians in the West began fighting fire with fire long ago. Those who fight the enemies of an open society by abandoning their own cultural openness have already lost.

The Muhammad caricatures are not a second Salman Rushdie affair. Rushdie had an inalienable right to defame his own Islamic culture. To treat one's own values and authorities with disrespect is the right, and in fact the duty, of literature and art, even though by doing so they incur hostility again and again. Rushdie takes his place in a long tradition of literary figures in the Muslim world who picked quarrels with Islam. Many of them have done so at the cost of prohibition, arrest, or their lives.

What the Danish editors were doing was something else entirely. They were needling a minority in their own country to incite a reaction that would serve as an excuse to marginalize that same minority still further. They were not defending the right to criticism and satire as the avant-garde of free speech. They were, and are, making fun of another culture. That is a whole different tradition in Europe, namely the tradition which has the least to do with humanism – in keeping with the political orientation of the Danish newspaper and the politicians that it supports. Their struggle is not only against Muslims but against everything that, after so many crimes and wars, has made Europe a wonderful place; against the values of tolerance, of reason, of social balance, of compromise as an achievement, of true secularism, which is based on equality between religions. Publishing caricatures at the expense of an already disadvantaged minority in one's own country is the opposite of Enlightenment. It was and is brute xenophobia.

We must also talk about some newspapers' negligent and sometimes intentionally one-sided and mendacious reporting – and not only in the Muslim world. From the beginning, they acted as if there was no division in the West between reporting and malevolence. Germany is not the world; it is not even Europe. In countries such as Greece and Poland, which also belong to the European Union, artists and authors who make fun of Christianity are regularly dragged into court. Just the week before last, a Muslim was sentenced to eight months' imprisonment in Rome because he took down the cross in his hospital room. Almost nothing was said about it in the media, no more than about the ordinary Muslim citizens who do not happen to live in the Neukölln borough of Berlin and who are aghast at their rioting brothers in faith.

Those who publish only hateful images of Muslims – masked men with machine guns, veiled female masses, headscarves photographed from behind in German schoolyards, faces distorted in screams, people praying, always in the brief instant in which they bring their foreheads to the ground, so that their hindquarters grin into the camera – must not be surprised if that hate escalates and becomes tangible. Much more insulting than the Danish caricatures are some books on the German best-seller lists, cover illustrations of *Der Spiegel*, and commentaries in the Axel Springer newspapers. When a politician such as Friedbert Pflüger, who wants to become mayor of Berlin, sings the extensive praises of Oriana Fallaci's best-seller *The Rage and the Pride*, in which Muslims – all Muslims, literally – are reviled as 'rats', then as a 'rat' you know where to think twice about living in future, depending on the election results: in this country's capital.

Anyone who tries to call attention to arguments, even to empirical knowledge, is immediately labelled a naive multiculturalist. If we believe the baiters in the German press, all the Islam scholars in German academia have been collectively taken in by the Islamists. German integration researchers are now suffering the same fate after having objected in an open letter in *Die Zeit* to the pseudoscientific discourse of German-Turkish best-seller authors who care nothing for confirmed empirical data. Readers of the indignant reactions to that open letter get the impression that Islamofascist brainwashing is going on in German universities. The commentators would rather listen to older gentlemen with horrifying anecdotes to tell about their Taliban friend, to German-Turkish women who can back up even the most absurd prejudices against Turkey with spectacular case studies, even to well-known Christian fundamentalists such as Hans-Peter Raddatz and Christine Schirrmacher, who have now become presentable in the respectable dailies.

To paraphrase Karl Kraus: the scandal begins when the media put an end to it – although Kraus referred to the police rather than the media. The current dispute over Muhammad caricatures will one day be used in media studies as an example of a perfect collaboration between Western and non-Western broadcasters in generating the mass hysteria they report on in just a few days. Whoever says anything about it becomes part of the screenplay in which everyone has to have their say, both the Islam critic and the representative Muslim, both the media critic and the journalist complaining about criticism of the media. This author can hardly wait to see what pigeonhole he'll be put in with the present text.

11

Relying Only on Strength Makes Israel Weaker

On the War in Lebanon

Süddeutsche Zeitung, 7 August 2006

Israel owes its survival to two constants: the support of the West and its strength in relation to its neighbours. The support of the Western community of nations is grounded in many different geopolitical and domestic interests, the feeling of cultural affinity, the work of educational institutions and lobbyists, economic relations, and more. Most of all, however, the West supports Israel for a deeply moral reason: because it is conscious of the suffering to which the Jews have been subjected. The particular morality of atonement that took its place in international politics after Auschwitz is probably unique in history.

To the new state's neighbours, however, this morality is not easy to understand. Neither do the Arabs have a comparable guilt, nor have they been broadly confronted in the course of their upbringing or in the media, as Europeans have, with the sorrowful history of the European Jews, and thus with the historic background of Israel. The hermetic nature of the Western legitimation of Israel is its critical fault down to the present. Except for the few who have acquired their education in the West, the people in the Middle East

– including hundreds of thousands of Palestinians waiting in refugee camps in the second or third generation – have little opportunity to comprehend, and hence to accept, the moral dimension of the reason for Israel's existence. At best, they can come to terms with the existence of Israel, not out of a motive of reconciliation, but out of acknowledgement of the enemy's often-proved superiority which seems to be cemented by the patronage of the West.

Since Ariel Sharon became prime minister, if not earlier, Israel has begun to rely less and less on morality and more and more on its own strength. It no longer wants to be the victim, because being the victim means being seen from a certain moral point of view: a victim can't simultaneously be a perpetrator, be stronger, be powerful. If the victim becomes powerful, its role as victim diminishes (hence the haste with which anti-Semites claim that Israel today is committing the crimes of the Nazis: to denounce the Jews' historic role as victims). But Israel wants normality, and that, in the case of a conflict that it experiences as existential, entails using power and military means just as resolutely, and just as ruthlessly, as other states do.

As long as the Israeli government is supported by the West, it can go on demonstrating its military superiority and maintain the concept of unilateral measures. If that support should fail to continue in its present form, however, all of Israel's strength will not help it. And because the neighbours will then see weakness, their acceptance of Israel's unshakeable existence – which has made great strides, stereotypical Israeli assertions notwithstanding – will diminish again. The anger of recent years will rekindle the anger of the past half century.

So far, the United States is giving Sharon's government free rein. But, in the long run, it will be impossible to ignore the doubts about such practically unconditional loyalty on

Washington's part if Israel continues its policy of absolute rigour until little remains of the moral stature of the former victims, which the West needs as a lasting basis for its solidarity. The historic reason will pale, and, in a not-too-distant future, the questions with which the conservative American political scientists John Mearsheimer and Stephen Walt unleashed fierce debate on both sides of the Atlantic will be raised in electoral campaigns and parliamentary discussions: what interest do we have in Israel? They will tally up costs and benefits: Israel has no oil and costs a lot of money. As it is constituted now, it creates unstable conditions in the Middle East and supplies terrorists with legitimation. To that extent, it endangers Western security. And so on. A purely interest-driven policy, like that which is generally pursued in regard to other states, would fundamentally change the West's relations with Israel. The shortfall from the cost–benefit account can be balanced out only by the West's humanitarian obligation towards the state of Israel. But that brings with it the requirement that Israel maintains its human face.

This expectation is an annoyance to the Israelis: hence Israeli intellectuals' constant references to much worse acts committed by the Russians in Chechnya and even the Americans in Iraq, to say nothing of Hisbollah and Hamas, which have murdered civilians indiscriminately. So why the uproar if the Israeli army – unintentionally, moreover – hits civilians?

Indeed, why? Why does Western public opinion have different standards for Israel from those applied to Hamas or Hisbollah, to Russia or to itself? Because the Western states, in the cases named – as is usual in politics – see their interests first and act accordingly. Most Western governments will quarrel with the United States as the leading power in the region only when it is unavoidable (the US is publicly criticized much more severely than Israel, by the way). Russia is too important as a partner country for relations to be endangered over Chechnya. And the terrorist acts of Hamas and Hisbollah? Of course they are dutifully condemned, but Hamas and Hisbollah are not supported financially or otherwise by the West. Thus the means of influence over them are limited to appeals, condemnations, sanctions. Israel on the other hand is closely allied with the West and thus much more subject to appeal, discussion and appraisal. Israeli intellectuals may complain, but it is precisely this special relationship, under the rule of morality, that guarantees Israel's existence.

For the West to revise its relationship to Israel seems farfetched at present – as long as the predictions are based on official statements and the commentaries in Germany's leading newspapers. If we have occasion to speak in private with the same politicians or commentators who formulate carefully considered criticism of Israel in their public statements, their indignation is often accompanied by a shrug: You can't say that out loud. And yet published opinion too has shifted significantly to Israel's detriment. Much of what is written about Israel today would have been unthinkable ten years ago. In other European countries, the criticism has taken on a severity that, in Germany, would be enough to incur the suspicion of anti-Semitism. But even among Israel's closest journalistic friends in Europe, there is more and more uncertainty expressed as to whether Israel can achieve its legitimate goal of security by a violence that seems increasingly mindless. If even these publications are no longer unreservedly supportive of Israeli government policy, we need not wonder at the opinions of artists, human rights activists and the population at large: it is only a matter of time before there will be increasing calls worldwide to boycott Israel.

As long as George W. Bush is president in Washington, Israel has no cause to worry unduly. But every conceivable successor in the Democrats' camp would build on Bill

Clinton's policy and work for a peace that does not stop at the unilateral boundary lines which reach far into the Occupied Territories. If Israel were then to react as dismissively as it has to all recent attempts to exercise influence, relations with Washington could also become noticeably cooler. Those who already see American interests being harmed in the Middle East would speak up still more loudly. Israel is dependent on morality for its survival.

The way to demonstrate morality, we often hear from Israel, is by not bombing civilians indiscriminately; Israel's reaction to such attacks should actually be much more rigorous. Supposing Israel were to lose its last scruples and lay waste large parts of Lebanon, the West Bank and Gaza to finally stamp out the threat – would that bring the Israelis even one step closer to living in peace? Sharon won the Israeli majority by promising security. His successor was elected because he promised to continue Sharon's policy. Today, Israelis' lives are more insecure than ever. They are being fired upon from the north and the south. The wrath that Israel stokes with its iron-fist policy, in conjunction with the lack of prospects among Palestinian youth, has created an army of potential attackers. The wave of terrorist attacks that Sharon's early acts first elicited and then suppressed by a massive use of force may have been only a harbinger of things to come. The Iraq War, roundly approved by Israel, has brought about a chaos in which the international jihadists are getting along wonderfully and Iran is increasingly dominating official policy. And in Iran meanwhile, and in Palestine almost simultaneously, extremists who, for the first time in a long time, are heavily and substantively questioning the existence of Israel in international politics have acceded to government functions. Hisbollah triumphs merely by continuing to exist. And Israel's global prestige has reached a low point.

Israeli sources rightly point out that Ariel Sharon and his heirs cannot be solely to blame for all of this, that the Arabs have behaved badly too, and that, with regard to the ethical justification of military force, it must be considered that the other side has sabotaged every peace initiative from Oslo to Gaza. But the distribution of wrong and right has long since become a secondary matter. What is critical, since the peace process first faltered with the murder of Yitzhak Rabin, and then came to a complete halt, are the results: they are devastating in every respect, and for all people in the region – Israeli or Arab – who long for normality, for a life without air strikes and rocket attacks, without suicide bombers in buses and without tanks at their doorstep. The fact that these people are still the majority is the only ground for hope.

12

WE ARE MURAT KURNAZ

Before Foreign Minister Steinmeier's Testimony
to the Bundestag Investigative Committee

die tageszeitung, 29 March 2007

That beard. And the hair. And the lock on his forehead, which is probably just a lock of hair, but looks greasy for some reason, or sweaty, probably because of the wild hairstyle. But especially that beard, that incredible beard, longer and frizzier than ... than ... and there's the association, although the other man's beard really looks quite different, practically sleek in comparison: longer and frizzier than bin Laden's beard. No, Murat Kurnaz's outward appearance is not apt to win him any sympathy in his German homeland. And yet it is this bearded young man with the shaggy hair whose story will reveal what our proclaimed values are really worth to us. We are Murat Kurnaz.

A constitutional democracy is no guarantee that everything that happens in a country is legal and proper. But it should guarantee that violations are punished and that victims see justice done. Before the law, and only before the law, everyone is equal, the president of the republic and the suspected radical. No one has to like Murat Kurnaz. Sympathy must not enter into it at all. He has rights – human rights – which are not negotiable and do not depend on his appearance, his religion or his itinerary. The very idea that an ethnic German or, let's say it right out, a blond-haired or a Christian man would remain in detention under torture while innocent, with the de facto consent of the German authorities, is absurd. In the case of a young man from Bremen with a Turkish passport, it is not.

The state, and uppermost that representative of the state who will report to the parliamentary investigative committee today, is guilty of racial discrimination. It happens, and by itself that would not be a reason to doubt the functioning of the rule of law. But it depends on what consequences this will have for those who contributed, in the name of Germany, to denying a person his fundamental rights for five years. It depends on days like this one.

There are two main arguments which the politicians and officials who were responsible at the time raise in their defence: Kurnaz, they say, was a security risk. And he was not a German. The first argument is correct, up to the year 2002. The initial suspicion against Kurnaz was justified. Even his lawyer does not contest this. But after that, not even circumstantial evidence could be discovered, not even under torture, that Kurnaz had connections to militant Islamists. That means that, from the year 2002 on, Murat Kurnaz was no longer a security risk. His detention, first in Afghanistan, then in Guantánamo Bay, was not only illegal but, from 2002 on, also groundless.

And even if Kurnaz had been the extremist the German authorities initially took him for, is it not the distinguishing feature of a constitutional democracy that it ensures due process even to those who oppose it? Instead, Kurnaz was first denounced by German officials, later repeatedly interrogated and, by his own testimony, which almost all members of the investigative committee have evaluated as credible, beaten and insulted by them. This proceeding is by itself so monstrous that it should be sufficient grounds to kick everyone involved out of office for good. All the scandals that have led to politicians' resignations in recent years are schoolboys' pranks in comparison.

The second argument that the Social Democrats put forward in defence of their foreign minister is Kurnaz's Turkish citizenship. Legally they may be right that Germany was not obligated to let Kurnaz re-enter the country, although he was born in Bremen (whether it was also right to ask the American colleagues for his passport to tear out his residence permit is another question – one which Frank-Walter Steinmeier would no doubt like to tear out of the dossier). But even if Kurnaz were a Chinese citizen and a resident of Kenya, we should have expected the German authorities – when they had the opportunity and offers on the table, no matter how specifically phrased – to seek an end to the illegal detention. Instead they did everything, including perverting the applicable immigration law, to prevent his return to Germany. They were well aware that Kurnaz would remain in the Americans' extralegal prison camp as a result. The record contains no statement that this was the least bit unpleasant to any of the people responsible at the time.

The whole argument that Murat Kurnaz lacked a German passport – as if one would have been any use to him as a suspected radical Islamist. Khaled El Masri is German: the succour that Germany brought him evidently consisted of punches in the face. Mohammad Zammar is also German, and yet there is no evidence that the German authorities made particular efforts to protect him from Syrian torture. On the contrary: documents of the CIA and FBI confirm the suspicion that the crucial information which led to his kidnapping by American agents came from Germany. Zammar too was interrogated by German officers under conditions that make a mockery of legal procedure. Abdel-Halim

Khafagy, on the other hand, is Egyptian, now seventy-four years old, but he lived for twenty-seven years unmolested in Bavaria, has several German children and, unlike Zammar, is what politicians like to describe as an example of successful integration. On 27 September 2001, he was abducted to a secret prison in Tuzla, Bosnia, and severely maltreated, according to agents of the German intelligence service BND. One agent received documents from American colleagues in Tuzla which were stained with Khafagy's blood. The German authorities rejected the petitions of Khafagy's lawyer time after time.

Oh – another argument that the Social Democrats cite in their defence stands out: the same Christian Democrat members of the Bundestag who are accusing the foreign minister today were those who then thought no action too harsh when it came to combating terrorism. That may be. One year after 9/11, the German government would certainly have been attacked by the Christian Democratic opposition if it had allowed the 'Bremen Taliban' to re-enter Germany. But at least it was a Christian Democrat, Angela Merkel, who has very quickly brought about what for the previous five years was alleged to be absolutely impossible and irresponsible: the return of Murat Kurnaz.

If there is hypocrisy at work, it is rather that of certain media whose sensational reporting about the 'Bremen Taliban' in particular and warnings against Islam in general helped to generate that atmosphere in which the authorities were afraid of Murat Kurnaz re-entering the country. But that's the way media are: they stoke resentments and they reflect resentments. It's all part of the job; after all, educating the public rarely raises sales at the newsagent's. Equally normal are reservations against Muslims, especially in view of the real danger of Islamist attacks. Resentments are a part of any society. What is foreign is considered a threat by most people and as enriching only by a minority. No one can be required to like Muslims. You are allowed to think them fearsome. You are allowed to write that they are fearsome and to insult their Prophet. That too is a defining characteristic of freedom, and it is one of the privileges from which the Muslims as a minority also benefit. But – and this is the crucial difference between opinions in society and the action of the state – the state must not take any part in the resentment. It must adhere to the principle of equality even if, and especially if, the mood in the society is otherwise.

For Muslims to be subjected to a dragnet investigation in Germany, or to be waved out of queues at the entry points to Germany, is not pretty; one may also think it's wrong – but it is provided for in law and it is at least understandable. After all, there is more danger of terrorist attacks by young Muslim men than by older Jewish women. To prevent attacks, democracies go to the limit of what is legally justifiable. Where the limit lies is decided by the courts in case of doubt. The cases of Kurnaz, El Masri, Zammar and Khafagy, however, are far beyond anything that is remotely consistent with the spirit and letter of the constitution. That is why they are far more worrying than, say, the wrangling over building mosques wherever they are proposed. The wrangling will pass, or else it will not; that is a problem for the Muslims. But here, the highest offices in the government have participated in violations of fundamental human rights. That is a problem for Germany. If that is tolerated, it would be a worse blow to the country's much vaunted system of values than a terrorist could ever deliver.

The consequences for the integration of migrants in Germany would also be disastrous. Or how are we in future supposed to persuade young Germans of Turkish or Arab background that they are not second-class citizens? And, to come back to the keyword hypocrisy in this context, the

Frankfurt judge who said in a divorce case that statutory trial separation should not be required of a Muslim's wife because the Quran sanctions wife-beating has been quite rightly criticized for it. But those who shout the loudest about the betrayal of Western values in that scandal are the quietest – no, they are perfectly silent – about victims of state injustice such as Murat Kurnaz.

Perhaps the legal judgement is different in cases in which the victim has German citizenship. The international warrant for the arrest of Khaled El Masri's kidnappers is a strong indication that German law enforcement is still largely immune to the virus that the so-called war on terror has released: defending the liberal order by abandoning it. But a government, not least one which has dedicated its foreign policy to the struggle against human rights violations and its domestic policy to the integration of migrants, is also subject to a political and moral judgement. This would be much more clement if any sign of regret were discernible on the part of those responsible. Why have Mr Steinmeier and Mr Schily not gone to Bremen to call on Murat Kurnaz and his mother? They could have explained to them the dramatic situation of those months that followed 9/11. They could have said that acting as they did was wrong in hindsight but, at the time, perhaps not entirely without reason under the circumstances. Frank-Walter Steinmeier is not someone who leaves observers or friends with an impression of hard-heartedness. If he had explained himself, face to face – Rabiye and Murat Kurnaz would hardly have refused the dialogue and the conciliatory photo for the press. They do not expect all that much. Their statements to date express more perplexity and pain than anger and accusation.

A word of sympathy would not have made up for their suffering, and yet it would have put the whole case in a different light. But no. The former home minister Otto Schily has had the insolence to declare in an interview that, if anyone ought to apologize, it was Kurnaz. All the others involved too assert that their actions were absolutely correct and would be the same in future under similar circumstances. Worse still, they pursue a fourth line of argument in their defence, the most despicable: the continued and systematic criminalization of Murat Kurnaz. Someone like that, they say, has got to be up to something. The responsible parties' strategy of painting the victim as a perpetrator, which is also that of the tabloid *Bild*, succeeds among some of the population, possibly on account of his appearance. Which brings us back to that beard.

It doesn't take any imagination to picture how his valiant lawyer, his frightened mother, perhaps even concerned talk-show producers have carefully or vehemently urged him to please go to the barber's before he addresses the public. Murat Kurnaz has refused. Perhaps this refusal has nothing to do with any stubbornness. Perhaps he is acting much more rationally than it seems. When all of this is over, when Murat Kurnaz is no longer the concern of any parliamentary commission and has done the round of all the talk shows – then maybe he will shave that beard off so he can go out again without being accosted in public. Then his untamed hair will have been just a disguise, and soon Murat Kurnaz will look like, well, not like the average German, but – with clean-shaven cheeks and a fashionable haircut – like one of us. But then we won't recognize him.

13

THE MESSAGE OF COLOGNE

The Discussion on Building a Grand Mosque

Süddeutsche Zeitung, 4 June 2007

First I had a visit from Markus Kerber, Home Minister Wolfgang Schäuble's section head who came up with the Conference on Islam. If I agree with the German government's man responsible for overseeing the integration of Islam on every point – our analysis of past omissions, our puzzlement at the statements of some Muslim spokespersons and our realization that patience is called for – things can hardly go wrong, I thought. In a sentimental moment towards the end of our conversation in the hip café La Pop, next door to the Turkish restaurant Doydoy with the plastic tablecloths and over the road from the shop with the model trains, to indicate just three of the parallel societies that are concentrated in my Cologne quarter of Eigelstein, I said to Mr Kerber and his assistant Mr Frehse, who is older than both of us and has no doubt seen a number of ministers come and go, I said, in forty, fifty years people will read in the chronicles: From 2006 on the Muslims made a home for themselves in Germany, and were considered a part of Germany, beginning with an initiative of the home minister, a Christian Democrat as it happened – and you are involved, and all of us together, the level-headed people in this country, we can do this. The others may rage, they may rouse the rabble, but things are in our hands. One day, when the editor-in-chief of one of the bourgeois papers is named Gülinaz or Mehmet, they'll come up with a different bugbear besides the supposed impossibility of integrating Muslims in Germany.

Then in the evening I attended the widely announced public consultation on the mosque to be built nearby in Ehrenfeld. We were all fearing the worst, especially after the escalation that the otherwise liberal daily *Kölner Stadtanzeiger* had set in motion with its reports and interviews. But, as it turned out, the hate preachers didn't get a chance. Four, five of them were ejected from the meeting, and the others were drowned out by the overwhelming majority of the eight hundred assembled citizens.

Of course concerns were expressed, and rejection too, but most of the objections were very specific and were articulated without foaming at the mouth. They had to do with traffic management, all the one-euro shops on Ehrenfeld's high street, the noise, the far too scant information provided by the builder, the height of the minaret – not the minaret per se. When the architect Gottfried Böhm projected a slide of the mosque's impressive and, contrary to what the newspapers had said, not at all Ottomanesque design, the people in the hall cheered – Germans. Just imagine it: the members of the ethnic majority not only tolerate a new minority's iconic building, but they say, Well, if a mosque looks as sumptuous as that, yes, we want it. Applause. The people have to pray somewhere. Applause. We can't keep saying they should integrate and at the same time expect them to keep their religion in the old factory lofts. Applause. We are Ehrenfeld! Cheering.

There is in Cologne a broad, liberal-minded mainstream, bordering sometimes on idealism, not least among people who wear only trousers with pleats. It has often struck me as amazing to live among such people, idealists if you like, but a thousand times more pleasant than ex-leftist converts to the clash of civilizations who no longer want to talk about having supported the Iraq War yesterday and today spit sound bites like those of the radical right onto the front pages in the name of Western freedom. I would a thousand times rather live among people who are always full of understanding whether or not it's called for, even where you might think, enough already.

Certainly the woman is right who complains that these Turks, although they're welcome to have their mosque as far as she's concerned, are always double-parking. The kids in the black BMWs upset me too. Cretin, I call after them, Scumbag, or, if they've taken my right of way in the cycle lane again, Bloody Turk. That's laughable almost, but the Afghan boy who beat up my daughter at school and is more than a match for the teachers and assistants because he doesn't seem to have learned respect for women at home, I didn't find him funny at all. Of course that's a problem. Only why does anyone expect that a 30 per cent proportion of immigrants and children of immigrants from mostly underdeveloped rural areas would not cause any problems for the indigenous 70 per cent?

Of course immigrants cause problems. But these problems need to be talked about – as they were at the public consultation. That – I could hardly believe my own eyes – was democracy at its finest. Everyone who speaks in a civil manner can express their opinion and will be answered, even if it goes on long past midnight. We have time, says the chair. Everyone will get their turn; procedure will be followed. You want to build a mosque? Do you have enough parking?

I had brought along Amir Hassan Cheheltan, the Iranian writer who is currently visiting Cologne under the auspices of the writers' exchange West–Eastern Divan. He was flabbergasted. What tolerance, he muttered again and again, what a developed country.

I saw how the young Turks glowed as they spoke their piece in better German than the troublemakers, how proud they were, how they thought, This is where we belong, including those who looked like black-BMW drivers (mine is blue and a station wagon, just so that's clear). A woman in a headscarf, her features Middle Eastern, her accent pure Rhineland, cried ecstatically that Cologne might maintain its world renown as a lesbian and gay centre (nothing less than world renown will do in Cologne) and also establish itself as a centre of religious diversity. At that prospect one can only raise one's eyebrows and nod: centre of sexual and religious diversity. That would be – no, that *is* – the message of Cologne. May it be heard – in all the world, in the homeland of my Iranian guest, or at the very least in the media, mosques and ministries of our republic.

14

Death on Wednesday?
The Trial of Ayatollah Boroujerdi in Tehran
Süddeutsche Zeitung, 19 June 2007

Someone cries, 'Break all cameras!' He does not say destroy or confiscate them. He says, Break them, just as Khomeini once commanded: Break them, the pens. The pens of Iranian poets, he meant. But this time perhaps the speaker means the cameras of the secret police.

A three-lane, one-way street in Tehran, at night; heavy traffic. Men between the cars hastily crossing from one pavement to the other. The cars advance only at a snail's pace. The flashing blue light of a green and white police car, a German-made saloon, parked facing against the traffic. Men on a moped stop. They must be the notorious plainclothes paramilitaries, quick with the truncheon. And in fact a bearded man with a truncheon runs through the frame. Screams, cries, unintelligible. Whole clusters of people are pushed back. 'Call the boys, tell them to get here quick,' someone shouts. Older women in white chadors stream into the street, their hands outstretched; also more and more young men, with and without beards, some of them with truncheons, others with baseball caps. The paramilitaries are hard to tell apart from the demonstrators. Cries: 'The master said we should assemble at the bottom of the lane.'

The master is Ayatollah Boroujerdi. The images on YouTube are dated 3 October of last year, and they show one of the attempts to arrest him. At that time, the people from the neighbourhood on Tehran's poor south side and Boroujerdi's followers were able to resist the paramilitaries. Five days later, however, the forces of the state succeeded in arresting the ayatollah. Eyewitnesses report that armoured vehicles were used, helicopters, tear gas, live ammunition. Five people died, they say, plus his aged mother, who did not survive the agitation. Of the five hundred people who were arrested, one hundred and twenty are said to be still in prison. Last week, according to reports, the prosecutor in the special court for the clergy requested the death penalty for Boroujerdi and seventeen of his followers. Some of the charges: endangering state security, disturbing the peace, questioning the Islamic order, claiming that Iran is ruled by a clerical dictatorship. The trial is being conducted in secret. The defence lawyers, who include the Nobel Peace Prize laureate Shirin Ebadi, have no contact with their clients. This makes it extremely difficult to obtain reliable information. Reports that Boroujerdi has already been sentenced to death do not seem to be correct, however. Sources close to him say that his sentence will be announced this Wednesday.

A speaker of the special court contradicted this statement, saying the verdict can be expected in two to three months. This is the first time a representative of the Iranian state has acknowledged that Boroujerdi is on trial at all. Up to now the media have not been allowed even to mention the ayatollah by name. 'A malcontent cleric' is the phrase used in the few notices that alluded to Boroujerdi's arrest. The reason is obvious: prominent clerics like him fill whole football stadiums with their followers at a word.

Ayatollah Seyyed Mohammad Ali Kazemeini Boroujerdi, a member of one of the most respected families of scholars in the country, is a radical secularist, but not because he advocates a reformed Islam corresponding to Western Enlightenment schools of thought on which, shortly before his death, the American philosopher Richard Rorty reported so hopefully. On the contrary, Boroujerdi is a traditionalist of the oldest school. He stands for the position of the Shiite orthodoxy – still widely held in the population – which has always advocated the separation of state and religion. Like those ultra-orthodox Jews who reject the state of Israel, they decry all human attempts to establish an order of divine justice on Earth. Instead they await the arrival of the Shiite messiah, the Mahdi, who alone has authority to bring about the kingdom of God on Earth. Until then, they adhere to a strict quietism: because all political rule is illegitimate in the absence of the Mahdi, the theologians should leave it to the lay authorities in order not to sully themselves. To these traditionalists, a man-made Islamic Republic is heresy.

Because they base their rejection of the existing model of the Iranian state on Shiite doctrine, they are especially dangerous and are persecuted as soon as they leave their secluded, scholarly lives, devoted mainly to ritual and ethical matters, to begin protesting against the state theologians. The regime in Tehran is particularly nervous because, since the fall of Saddam Hussein, quietist Islam, of which Grand Ayatollah Sistani is also an exponent, has been able to reorganize in the centres of Shiite theology in Iraq, out of Tehran's reach. The repression in Iran has sharply increased in the past several months; the security agencies continue to arrest numerous dissidents, including women's rights activists from the One Million Signatures campaign for a reform of Iranian law. The confrontation with the West that President Ahmadinejad pursues is accompanied at home by steadily increasing pressure on Iranian society.

Later in the video, we can see how Ayatollah Boroujerdi appears before the crowd that has formed in front of his house. He is wearing only a white garment, not the black turban that identifies him as a descendant of the Prophet. For a few seconds one might think he has just woken up. His hair is uncombed, his long grey-black beard dishevelled. Then one realizes that the cleric has put on his burial shroud, the plain white cloth in which Muslims are buried. See, it means, I have no fear. He has already been arrested several times in the nineties. His father, also an ayatollah, died under mysterious circumstances in 2002 during treatment in hospital. The Nour Mosque where his son buried him was seized by the state and the tomb desecrated. Boroujerdi accuses the rulers not only of arresting and torturing numerous followers: female family members, he says, have been sexually assaulted in prison and filmed in degrading situations.

Later still, Boroujerdi is holding a microphone. *Besmellah-e rahman-e rahim*, he begins his address, 'In the name of God, the Merciful, the Compassionate,' and he addresses his neighbours, apologizing for the disturbance: 'You should know that agents of the secret police stormed our house an hour ago. You should know that the security agencies have blocked all approaches and have organized to attack us and to kill me. You should know that we are against the mixing of politics and religion. We do not want to inflict injustice on people in the name of religion. We do not want to destroy the Iranian nation in the name of religion.' Twenty, thirty of his followers are arrested every day and taken to Block 209 of Evin Prison, the torturers' block. Offers to tempt him to back down are futile, he says: 'The Boroujerdis do not deal with any government.'

Many people today forget that the founder of the Islamic Republic, Ayatollah Khomeini, was perceived by his theological colleagues before the revolution as a radical reformer, as a liberation theologian, because he wanted to realize the messianic promise in real, earthly history. Khomeini was prevented from publicizing his political Islam by none other than an ancestor of the imprisoned cleric, Grand Ayatollah Hussein Boroujerdi – until that Boroujerdi's death in 1964. And Khomeini once said himself that his chief enemy was neither the shah nor the United States but the traditional Shiite clergy. The charges against the present Boroujerdi are the most recent outbreak of a bitterly fought fraternal struggle that has dominated Shia Islam for the past fifty years.

At the end of the video, Boroujerdi addresses the state forces directly: 'Are you here to serve the nation or to kill the children of the nation? Are you here to fight poverty and drug addiction or to annihilate the descendants of the Prophet?' His voice grows increasingly strident. He raises his left and right hands alternately as he speaks. 'Islam commits no injustice. The Prophet is not an oppressor. God does not steal the people's bread.' He tells the security forces, who at this moment are aiming their rifles at him and his followers, that he and they are not willing to sell out Islam. 'O people of the neighbourhood, you shall bear witness that the Boroujerdis are willing to die so that the true Islam remains. Are we terrorists?'

With his turban, his long garment and the beard that covers much of his face, Boroujerdi fits the West's image of hate preachers or terrorist leaders; so do his tone of voice, his anger. He is not an eloquent intellectual like the philosopher Abdolkarim Soroush, not a well-dressed moderate like the former president Khatami. The face of Islam that he embodies is not more smart than that of his enemies who want to kill him. Boroujerdi is common or garden Islam: conservative to reactionary on most social issues, patriarchal, but also secular and resolutely non-violent. It still exists, after almost thirty years of political re-education in the country's theological seminaries. If even these ayatollahs, whose whole mentality, upbringing and theological tradition are apolitical, are now protesting, if they are preaching that the red line has been crossed, how far must the Islamic Republic have gone?

15

Rejection of Europe

The Swiss Referendum on the Prohibition of Minarets

Süddeutsche Zeitung, 11 December 2009

If any political unit in the world besides the United States of America offers religious and ethnic minorities the prospect of equal participation, it is a united Europe. Unlike the nation-state, Europe in the emphatic sense designates a canon of values which one can profess – or not profess – regardless of one's nation, ethnicity, religion or culture. That does not eliminate differences – on the contrary, Europe is not an extended kind of nation-state but a mode of politically defusing differences in order to preserve them. Who is part of the European 'we' is determined not by their grandparents' birthplace but by their own conception of the present.

The Swiss referendum on the prohibition of minarets is in several respects a break with central principles of this European project of a secular, transnational, multi-religious and multi-ethnic intentional community that has grown out of the Enlightenment and the French Revolution. It has been written many times in recent days that the new clause in the Swiss constitution violates the right to the free exercise of religion. It has also been noted that the minaret ban discriminates against a certain faith and is thus incompatible with the principle of equality enshrined in the European canon of values. Less often mentioned is the most serious taboo violated by the referendum, regardless of its outcome: it makes fundamental rights, the fundamental rights of a minority no less, negotiable in a democratic plebiscite – which means they are no longer fundamental rights.

It is in the nature of taboos that they lead us into temptation to break them. When violations of a taboo are no longer so named, and hence censured, the taboo has been socially broken. The reactions of the many representatives of European governments who have spoken cautiously, soliciting understanding, are therefore disastrous. Those who now seek to allay fears are provoking an even greater storm. The same arguments that have been fielded in favour of the minaret ban will now be applicable to prohibitions of all other forms of Islamic presence, or any culturally foreign presence, in public spaces. This concerns not just Muslims; it concerns all Europeans. The right-wing populists and their formerly liberal, now neo-conservative forerunners in the media, who show the zeal of converts in Germany as elsewhere, may be attacking Islam, but their real target is the European project. It is no coincidence that they are uniformly sceptics towards, if not opponents of, the process of European unification and that their economic ideas are neoliberal, which is to say opposed to the social legacy of the European founding fathers and mothers.

Before the Swiss referendum, there was a discussion going on in many European countries about the problems of integration, about Islam and about equality specifically in Muslim immigrant milieus, and it will go on after the referendum as well. Wherever Muslims build a mosque, wherever they want to publicly express or practise their faith, they are exposed to this discussion. That is not always pleasant to them, and it may not always be a fair debate, but it is unavoidable in a polity that sets very, very broad limits on free speech, for good reasons. The demographic change in the Western European societies within a single generation has been tremendous, perhaps even unprecedented in history. The discussion is hitting the continent today with such force because the real conflicts, and also the imagined ones, which accompany that demographic change have not been addressed. The discourse is part of a necessary process of familiarization and cultural assimilation which is beginning decades too late.

The answer cannot be to silence certain opinions or to impose taboos against discussing certain problems which are correctly or mistakenly associated with Islam. But it is necessary that the debate be conducted on the basis and in the context of the European canon of values as it is anchored in the constitutions of most European countries and in the European Convention on Human Rights. That is why the constant comparisons with the situation of religious minorities in Islamic countries which have been cited in defence of the Swiss vote are self-debasing – a cultural and moral capitulation. In spite of all the failings, freedom of religion, which is more real in Europe than in most other parts of the world, has been and is still one of the features that distinguish Europe from countries such as the Islamic Republic of Iran and Saudi Arabia, and is one of the reasons why Turkey is still not European at this moment. The fundamentalism which the anti-minaret campaigners ostensibly oppose would triumph if Europe itself were to become fundamentalist.

Switzerland too – whose constitution, unlike Germany's 'Basic Law', does not individually list the non-negotiable fundamental rights nor establish a constitutional court – like other democracies, Switzerland too has a safety mechanism to guard against undemocratic decisions, namely in the form of the European Court of Human Rights in Strasbourg.

Switzerland has voluntarily submitted to its jurisdiction by signing the European Convention on Human Rights. According to everything written by legal experts in recent days, the interpretations of the minaret which the proponents of a ban have cited to mask their proposed violation of the right to free exercise of religion – calling it either a purely political symbol or one that is not originally Islamic – will not stand up in Strasbourg. After the court's expected judgement, Switzerland would then be at the same crossroads constitutionally to which it has already come as a society: will it accept the judgement, or will it leave the Council of Europe and with it the community which upholds the philosophical legacy of the Enlightenment?

Nevertheless, it would be absurd to stand idly by in anticipation of the decision from Strasbourg. If the conflict which has arisen between the manifestation of a majority's will and a minority's fundamental rights is brought to a purely juridical resolution, it will return in greater political volatility – in the form of right-wing populist parties winning not just a third of the votes in legislative elections but majorities. In other words: those who insist that fundamental rights are not negotiable in the democratic process should still do everything possible to ensure that they are always supported by a majority. If the social consensus is permanently dissolved, the courts will no longer be able to patch it up.

It has often been said recently that the population's fears of Islam should be taken seriously. In one respect, that is always true, and yet, in the specific case of the minaret referendum, it clouds the fact that those fears have been purposely stoked in an elaborate campaign. Only that explains why such fears are strongest where the fewest Muslims live: in the rural areas and also in certain wealthy, upper-class districts. And, speaking of fears, it is telling that hardly any European leader has had even one word to say about the fears of those who have just been stamped second-class citizens in a European country. What kinds of flyers and what integration summits are supposed to persuade them in future to feel themselves a part of European societies? When Switzerland's largest and, thanks to its leader, best-financed party advertises with posters that explicitly refer to the symbolism of the Nazi magazine *Stürmer*, when its official website offers an online game in which players can shoot down imams, when formerly liberal newspapers apply the argumentative structure and certain stereotypes of Nazi propaganda to Muslims, then it is not only Islam which has a problem with hate preachers.

The Western variant of fundamentalism – in which ideology is based on cultural rather than religious or ethnic tradition – has become a challenge in European internal politics, as indicated by the growth of right-wing populist parties in further countries, including Austria, Italy, Denmark and the Netherlands. In all of these countries, the conflict with those parties, and with the journalists who pave their way in the media, is being waged defensively. The traditional parties, especially the conservative ones, downplay the dangers that this current poses to the European project, gradually adopt its rhetoric, and in many cases even involve it in government. The strategic calculation that this would lead to moderation among the right-wing populists or cost them voters has never yet worked out anywhere. On the contrary, the rise of right-wing populism is absent from precisely those countries which have worked politically in the past few years to shape integration instead of populistically exploiting upheavals. In Sweden, Spain and Germany, for all the necessary disagreement over the details, there is a basic consensus between the established parties that migrants must be included in the body politic rather than marginalized for the sake of anticipated election results.

It is obvious, and it can certainly be communicated at the polls, that social and cultural conflicts cannot be resolved through prohibitions and discrimination, which only exacerbate the social segregation that is said to be so offensive. Consequently, taking people's concerns about immigration seriously cannot mean anticipating and satisfying the right-wing populists and legislating invisibility for foreign cultures. Rather, the fears must be defused by demonstrating more realistic prospects and managing solutions to concrete problems – through language learning in kindergarten, women's shelters, massive investment in education, measures to combat tendencies towards ghetto formation in the cities, and training imams locally, to name just a few examples.

The instruments of the building code are also an important factor in this regard. They can ensure the integration of hitherto unaccustomed religious architecture in the urban environment: not simply by permitting only the most inconspicuous buildings imaginable but, more convincingly, by an aesthetically appealing, contemporary Islamic architecture that embraces and extrapolates European styles. But, most of all, to renew the European social contract a generation after the historic immigration wave of the 1950s and '60s, a lot of persuading will be necessary on all levels of society: in the schools, the media, the parties, government agencies, factories, churches, mosques, associations and families. Civic education, after all, is our legacy from the Enlightenment.

16

A STATE WITHOUT A PEOPLE

The Recent Mass Protests in Iran

Die Zeit, 30 December 2009

Those who demonstrate for freedom in Iran in these days, in spite of the bellicose threats and the brutality of the Revolutionary Guards, are consciously risking their lives. These men and women – and it must be mentioned that there are many women protesting – are taking the risk of stepping in front of the rifles of snipers who need no further orders to shoot. These men and women know that the paramilitaries have no other ambition than to bring down their clubs on as many skulls as possible. These men and women have experienced more than once what it is like to get caught in a cloud of tear gas; they have screamed with pain, nausea and rage. These men and women are aware that they may be tortured and raped, but they will certainly be sent down from university and ruin their professional future if they are arrested or identified in the video recording of a surveillance camera. These men and women fear that revenge may be taken on their parents or siblings.

And nevertheless, every time the green opposition has called for demonstrations in recent months, tens of thousands of people have dared to march. Every one of them has relatives, acquaintances, colleagues, neighbours, schoolmates, fellow students and teachers who fear for their safety. Every time, the regime announces that the next day of protest will be dealt with more harshly. Every time, they still dare to march. Every time, there are more of them – at the burial of Grand Ayatollah Montazeri in Qom a week ago Monday, there were half a million. And, every time, their slogans have grown more radical, so that their protest today is no longer directed against suspected election fraud but against the whole system. The fact that the security forces, although they stop at nothing, are unable to suppress the protest marches must be a more lasting shock to the regime than the mass demonstrations of last summer, which were tolerated at first. Not only the demonstrators, but also the servants of the regime have relatives, acquaintances, colleagues, neighbours – and the security forces will not always be able to repress the thought of them when they look through their rifle sights.

Not the bloodiest, but probably the most surprising image of last weekend was that of the state's thugs storming the private mosque of the state's founder, Ayatollah Khomeini, nothing less than a sacred shrine of the Islamic Revolution. They were not chasing some Western-oriented politician but literally wanted the head of Muhammad Khatami, a theologian with the black turban of the descendants of the Prophet, who was president of the Islamic Republic of Iran until four and a half years ago and was giving a religious sermon in the mosque. The other enemies of the state today are also statesmen of yesterday: Mir-Hossein Mousavi is a former prime minister, Mehdi Karroubi a former president of the parliament, Grand Ayatollah Saanei a former chairman of the Guardian Council. Most of the prisoners who are shown on state television giving sham confessions in pyjamas and plastic slippers are former cabinet ministers, members of parliament, leaders of the 1979 embassy occupation; there is also a vice-president of Iran from the years 1997 and 2005,

Mohammad Abtahi. Thus the revolution is putting itself on trial.

And thus it is no coincidence that the event which set off the current protests against the Iranian theocracy was the death of Grand Ayatollah Montazeri. The reason was not only what he had said – his thundering against the tyranny, denying the leader of the revolution's legitimacy, condemning the construction of an atomic bomb, and asserting that all citizens of Iran had equal rights regardless of their faith, explicitly including the Baha'i minority. The reason was also *who* had said all that: not some young rabble-rouser, not a secular intellectual, but the highest Shiite theologian of his time and Khomeini's closest ally, until 1989 his designated successor.

Nevertheless, nothing could be more mistaken than to reduce the current unrest to an internal power struggle within Iran's Islamic establishment. The confrontation between the former comrades is merely the most visible sign of a social conflict in which, on one side, a steadily growing majority is tired of being patronized in the name of ideology and, on the other side, a minority feels obligated to defend the existing order, which it has declared divine. The fissure runs through almost all areas of Iranian society. It is visible in business, among a developing, internationally thinking elite who have a different worldview from that of traditional merchants in the bazaar. The fissure divides women into mothers who have never learned anything but housework and millions and millions of daughters whose resolve to run their own lives is made all the stronger by the state-decreed inequality. The fissure divides the generations, and it runs through many families in which the children don't understand why their parents were once willing to die for this system in the war against Saddam Hussein's Iraq, while the parents are horrified that their children so radically reject what they fought and sacrificed so much for. But the conflict is most acute and most manifest at the core of the Islamic Republic: within the clergy.

The discussions that began in the early 1990s in religious-philosophical journals and theological seminaries, and reached the most widely circulated daily newspapers before they were banned, are aimed at a change that would separate politics from religion and derive the government's authority from the people, not God. This reform of Islam is based on a philosophical and historical development that could not be happening faster and could not be more profound. It is a genuine product of Iranian culture, the collective experience of Iranian society. This gives it permanence, substance and an intellectual incisiveness that is unthinkable in most countries of the Muslim world today. In the struggle for separation of state and religion, Iranian society is going through an intellectual change that the Western-oriented Arab dictatorships, in their zeal for modernization, have neglected, perhaps even prevented. This learning process could be something to be glad of were it not for the immense human, political and social cost to the country, and were the possibility of a civil war not so real – a civil war in the sense of a war against the state's own citizens.

There is an irrefutable reason why the strictly theocratic model of the Iranian state cannot last: the rulers have lost the society. In the early 1980s, Khomeinism had a strong, although not unlimited, support in the centres of popular Shiite religion – that is, in the small and medium-sized towns and in the bazaars and the poorer quarters of the big cities. At the same time, Khomeini's ideology has always been alien both to the urban middle and upper classes and to a large part of the rural population, whose religiousness is very diverse, and sometimes only rudimentary. Although the first group could be called cosmopolitanized and the second traditional – nevertheless, they share an attitude towards religion that is eminently secular: most members of these groups see Islam as a private matter, not as a political standard or a source of the state's laws. The rural population have never had a share in political decision-making in the Islamic Republic; the bourgeoisie only in the very beginning. Few of them support the system, but they hardly endanger it either. In the course of the 1990s, however, it became progressively clearer that even those segments of the population whose loyalty gave the Islamic Republic its foundation had long since turned away in droves from their own political elite. Those who are marching for freedom in these days can no longer be assigned to a particular social background. They are the people.

The *ancien régime* may, in the days to come – and perhaps for a few years yet – persuade itself with tooth and nail that it still has a chance. But in fact it has already lost. It has lost because the society's ideas, those of the majority, have already advanced beyond the paternalism, the instrumentalization of religion and, for that matter, any ideological saturation of the public sphere. The former statesmen who are now enemies of the state are responding to this progress; they are not its initiators. Because that was not understood in the West, the revolution of the Revolution which began before the election of the reformist president Khatami went unseen for a long time, was written off after the first setbacks, forgotten with the inauguration of the hard-liner Ahmadinejad, and pronounced dead after the violent suppression of the protests last June. Social change takes place more slowly than the election of a different government or the revolution of a political system – but, when it happens, it is irreversible.

Both the West and the East have some experience of actually existing ideologies. In 1979 Iran became the first state in the Muslim world to undertake the experiment of Islamism. Today the Iranians are fighting, in some respects vicariously for many societies of the Middle East, what may be the last great battle to correct the error of the last century: the belief in a salvation arising from a political doctrine.

17

Allianz Lecture on Europe
Deutsches Theater, Berlin, 23 October 2011

We hear on all sides that Europe is in a crisis, its most severe crisis since the Second World War. But the strange thing is: it is a long time since Europe has had as many advocates as today, or such prominent ones. In the face of the immense financial transactions, the stock market crash and the deterioration of the euro, one might have expected the Euroscepticism that exists among the population to take a firmer hold of politics and the media than ever. But even politicians and commentators who have stood out in the political debates on Europe in recent years by their business-like attitude, indeed their demonstrative emphasis on national interests, are now discovering Europe as the defining political issue of their lives and are warning in remarkably emotional terms against letting the European Union fail. It almost seems as if the world spirit, which was already European as early as Hegel, has played one of its tricks again: plunging the European Union into a debt crisis so that the appeal for more Europe will be heard before it is too late. Economic governance, a uniform tax on financial transactions, intervention in national budgets, harmonization of tax law – what a year or two ago were the demands of scattered Europe enthusiasts suddenly seems to be what is possible and necessary.

A person like me, whose political situation was made possible by the European project, is of course glad, deep down, at the sudden willingness to break free of thinking in terms of nation-states, at least for purposes of economic policy. And yet the affirmations of Europe seem oddly hollow: Europe, yes – but why, really? In any case, it is nearly impossible to awaken a new enthusiasm for the European project among the population – or confidence, or merely understanding, for that matter. On the contrary: in diametrical opposition to the trend in published opinion, scepticism towards Europe is growing in opinion surveys. This also expands the political space that staunchly nationalist actors can occupy, whether in politics or the media, but always with the pretence of breaking taboos which every form of populism assumes: We're only saying – in fact we're only asking a question: Europe, yes – but why, really?

The argument that the European Union has brought together nations that were once enemies and brought to the continent a peace that was hardly thought possible has become a cliché heard in every political speech on Europe. The argument is not wrong; it has merely lost its effectiveness seventy-six years after the end of the Second World War. No one honestly believes that the member countries of the European Union would make war on one another again if the political federation were to disintegrate. So what remains that can persuade people of the necessity of Europe? If we study the speeches given in the most recent debate on Europe in the Bundestag, the remaining argument in favour of Europe is mainly the economic and strategic advantage of a common market. 'If the euro fails, Europe fails,' in Chancellor Merkel's memorable phrase.

Is that how it is? Is the euro really the foundation on which Europe rests? Was there not something more? And could it not be that precisely this shift, this reduction of the

European project to the economy, that we encounter daily in the apologetics of the present debt crisis, is itself the cause, or one important cause, of the crisis, of the lack of democratic participation, of persuasiveness, of legitimacy? It may be that shares and exports would fall without the common currency. But are persuasive economic benefits the reason why we believe in Europe? No, the euro is not the goal, the reason and the motor of two hundred and fifty years of European unification, which at its heart is a political project and in its origins a project in the history of philosophy. Even the founding fathers of the European Union – just read the earliest visions of a Jean Monnet, of a Robert Schuman – the founding fathers were thinking of more than just coal and steel. The European Coal and Steel Community was the means of bringing together the nations that were enemies. It was not the goal. Its ultimate goal went far beyond not only an economic union but beyond Europe. In his own words, Monnet was striving for 'an organization of the world which would permit the full development of its resources, distributing them equitably among humanity, in order to create a condition of peace and happiness throughout the world.' Monnet's statement dates from 1943. How realistic might the proposal of a political union of the European countries have sounded then? A common currency, a common parliament, open borders from North Cape to Gibraltar? And yet Monnet turns out to have been a realist when, in the middle of the Second World War, he forged plans for a democratically constituted community of the European countries, Germany included. It was the grand vision of a more peaceful and more just world that gave him the power and the imagination to move Europe forward in tiny steps, with coal, steel, and great persuasiveness.

I am probably a member of the more informed, to some extent politically educated part of the population. I listen to news radio while brushing my teeth; at breakfast I read one of the better newspapers; and I often fall asleep at night reading a political book. And yet I have not the faintest inkling whether all of these financial stimuli and bailouts and transactions that are being whipped through the European parliaments on a scale that is simply inconceivable to laypersons – whether these measures are right, whether they will achieve the advertised effects, whether there are realistic alternatives. I suspect that many if not most of the members of those parliaments have at best an inkling of what they are deciding now, and what the consequences will be.

If even the German minister of finance admits – and his doing so seems at least honest to me – that he is flying by the seat of his pants, then how should we, sitting in the back of the plane, know whether we are going the right way? I can only say that I have a general confidence, in part by necessity, that some of the active players are the people most likely to be able to make the right decisions. To pursue the finance minister's metaphor: when the pilot is steering us through dense clouds, that is not the time to seize the controls. So let us hope that the euro remains with us, that Greece is able to stabilize and that holidays in Switzerland become affordable again. But can we in all seriousness believe that the course corrections now initiated, which are purely matters of economic policy, will remedy the European Union's two fundamental disparities? Namely, that the economic process of unification was not accompanied by a political one, nor has the enlargement of the union been accompanied by a consolidation. The European Union has twenty-seven member countries today, but it is based on a political and legal construct that is so weak that it would not even serve as a foundation for a functioning marriage. How is this enormous territory supposed to be governed if twenty-seven heads of government, cabinets and parliaments have to be persuaded before every decision? And how are the citizens of Europe supposed to be confident in the first place if they feel their opinion is not wanted, if they are not being included in a democracy nor even properly informed?

The crisis of the European Union today is not a debt crisis. The debts are the expression and the consequence of a political crisis. If the political community is treated with such negligence, indifference, sometimes even contempt, as the heads of government and a good deal of public opinion have shown in recent years, we must not be surprised at such a disaster as we are experiencing now. If the larger member states – including and especially the Federal Republic of Germany – put their national interests first in the course-setting decisions of recent years, then a transnational structure such as the European Union must fall apart sooner or later. If the leading posts in Europe are intentionally filled with politicians of no charisma or authority – Lady Ashton! – whom no one will remember in a few years, just to ensure that the national leaders retain the limelight, then the lack of leadership is the logical result. If fundamental decisions about the future of five hundred million people are not taken by the competent, much less the democratically legitimate institutions, but more and more frequently in preliminary bilateral talks, it is no wonder the people lack confidence. If Europe's reaction to its political crisis is purely an economic one, it will not master the emergency.

The decline of the European Union can be dated fairly precisely. It began with the transition from the generation whose political consciousness was formed within sight of the horrors of the war to the generation responsible today, who did not suffer through the existential necessity of European reconciliation. This is not by any means limited to the political decision-makers. The cool-headedness, indeed the indifference, with which Europe has been treated by many heads of government in recent years is an expression of an apathy in society. Let us just look at who governs Europe today; look at Rome, look at Prague, Budapest, Paris – do we see there heads of government who embody the European project, the Europe of the Monnets and Schumans? Do we see the Europe of a Victor Hugo, a Stefan Zweig? Let us look at The Hague, at Copenhagen, where 'right-wing populist' parties which are not only xenophobic but also resolutely anti-European participate in government without causing an uproar of outrage. What else should we expect from such governments besides wilful sabotage of European unity? Or let us look at Berlin, where the chancellor's and the foreign minister's most recent political pledges to Europe are gratifying, and perhaps subjectively credible, but terribly late in coming. Where was the forcefulness when it was time to fight for a European constitution? Where were the passionately delivered arguments the last time the top European posts had to be filled? European foreign policy has deteriorated into a joke, although European engagement is needed more urgently than ever, in the Middle East for example. The protection of refugees – one of the groundbreaking achievements of the European legacy – has become nothing but protection *from* refugees, so that today there is explicit talk of 'combating refugees'. Combating refugees! The very expression is a total reversal of everything Europe, in the emphatic sense, stands for. But that is not all, nor even the worst. Worse still is the fact that no one is even upset by such an expression out of the mouth of a German chancellor.

It is thus not a slip but the logical consequence of purely interest-driven politics that Europe cooperated so shamelessly with North Africa's dictators – no, Europe grovelled at the feet of North Africa's dictators, before the Arab Spring took it by surprise. We had to remain in dialogue with the Mubaraks, the Ben Alis, the Gaddafis, they said; that is how diplomacy works. But was it still European diplomacy to accept the invitation of Hosni Mubarak, as Nicolas Sarkozy did, to an Egyptian holiday, to send police reinforcements to Zine el-Abidine ben Ali to club peaceful demonstrators, or to kiss the hand of Muammar al-Gaddafi, as Silvio Berlusconi did, in front of the cameras of the global media? His hand! European foreign policy has never been free of cool, calculating and self-interested realpolitik. But in recent years, instead of Europe standing for the spread of human rights in the world, human rights have had to be defended against Europe. In 2010, the assault on the Bastille was closer to Tahrir Square than to the Elysée. Whether the recent engagement in Libya marks a rethinking or was only a tactic to secure access to mineral resources remains to be seen.

If I criticize Europe, it is not because I reject Europe. I criticize Europe because I believe in Europe as a political space, perhaps even the one political space, in which people of different ethnicities, faiths, languages, genders, sexual orientations and beliefs can live in equality and on the basis of secular, democratic constitutions. And, more concretely: I also believe in the European project of unity, in this so lacklustre, clumsy, lumbering, bureaucratic European Union with all its administrative absurdities that lend themselves to cheap sarcasm, the Europe of the lunch box regulation, the light bulb ban and the hopelessly overtaxed translation service. The European Union, together with its precursors, is the greatest political achievement on this continent in the past century, if not in all of European history. It has not only brought peace among nations that were once opposed in hatred and belligerence, it has also brought the continent democracy, the rule of law and prosperity. For Europe is not just a project for peace. It is also a project for freedom: it was the bond with the European project that first allowed democracy to succeed in Germany; it was the pressure from Europe that contributed crucially to overturning the dictatorships in the south of the continent – as we too easily forget today – in Spain, Portugal, Greece; it was the prospect of belonging to Europe that later stimulated the Eastern European states, and most recently the Balkan countries and Turkey, to begin democratic reforms. To advocate for Europe today, it is not enough to point to our own economic or geopolitical advantage. Such a purely utilitarian argument not only goes against the core of the European idea, which is an idealistic one, the idea of a more just world. Those who reduce the European Union to economic advantage find themselves empty-handed as soon as the bottom line takes a turn for the worse. That is exactly what we are observing in the political rhetoric of recent days: the helpless search for a calculation that makes the trillions in transfers seem somehow plausible. But what if the financial aid is simply not economically profitable – if it is really aid, and not investment?

To find an answer, it is a good idea to go back, not to the beginning of the European Union, but to the beginnings of the European project. The project of a united Europe goes back historically to the French Revolution, and philosophically to the Enlightenment. The essential currents of its founding ideas were aimed not at bringing about peace between warring nations but at opposing the nationalism that was the politically dominant force in most of the European countries, opposing the ideal of a national unity of culture, language, religion and blood. It is thus no wonder that the advocates of the European idea included disproportionately many Jewish intellectuals and members of ethnic or linguistic minorities who were personally affected by chauvinism within the nation-states. Many of the pioneering thinkers of Europe in the nineteenth century were arrested or forced to flee their homes: Ernst Moritz Arndt, Arnold Ruge, Percy Bysshe Shelley, Friedrich von Gentz, Giuseppe

Mazzini, Joseph von Görres, Victor Hugo, Heinrich Heine. Well into the twentieth century, it was primarily writers, poets, intellectuals who espoused pan-Europeanism: in the German-speaking countries, the Mann brothers and Klaus Mann, Alfred Döblin, Joseph Roth, Stefan Zweig, Hugo von Hofmannsthal and Hermann Hesse, to name only a few. They too were expelled or banished, died in exile or in the death camps. That means that the political and in many cases biographical motivation to conceive of a united Europe was not the experience of the war but that of national chauvinism. Thus Europe remained for a long time the vision of a minority, a vision of poets and philosophers. Only when the dangers of nationalism had become obvious in two world wars was the idea of a united Europe politically viable. The appeal to peace was practically the prayer of invocation at the birth of European unification. But if it is taken for granted that we live in peace, the prayer becomes a commonplace, and that is what we perceive today.

Hardly anyone disputes that European unity has brought peace to the continent. But a political belief for which people are willing to work, and to make sacrifices, does not arise simply from reading history books; it comes from personal experience. It is rooted in the here and now, and its focus is not on the past but on the future: what society do I want to live in? Today the European project of peace would do well to rediscover the project of freedom that it originally was.

What society they want to live in who reject the European project can be studied with some precision. It is visible in the programmes of the right-wing populist parties; it is visible in the politics of those countries in which they are already included in the government; in the more restrictive immigration laws; the aspiration to unilateralism in foreign policy; the resistance against supranational institutions, and most vehemently against the Strasbourg court; the plea to reintroduce border checks; the rejection of the right to political asylum; the rhetoric of contempt towards minorities, including sexual minorities by the way; the revocation of all solidarity, whether with the weaker members of their own societies or with the poor people of the world, and also with future generations, as manifested in the denial of climate change and the resistance against any ecologically oriented policy; the break not only with the political legacy but also, and especially, with the social legacy of Europe's founding fathers. What we call right-wing populism today is the same in its essential characteristics as that very national chauvinism to which the European idea was opposed from its formation in the nineteenth and early twentieth centuries.

Yes, nineteenth-century nationalism also spoke of freedom, just as the right-wing populism of today and its mostly neoliberal enablers in the media appeal to freedom when they rant against the European institutions as a colonial yoke. But both the ethnic-national and the individualistic notions of freedom lack an essential element of the Enlightenment: the element of solidarity, as we most often call it today; of fraternity, as it was called in 1789; or of loving thy neighbour, in the Hebrew tradition. This element distinguishes the modern from the ancient concept of freedom. Freedom in the polis refers exclusively to the polis itself: to its own citizens; and the exploitation of others as slaves is in fact constitutive for this freedom as it frees the citizens from the burden of their daily livelihood. To Aristotle, only leisure makes possible the freedom to act politically. Hence the ancient concept of equality is not, and cannot be, essentially universal. The crucial revision which the concept of freedom has gradually undergone in contact with the biblical tradition consists precisely in its universalism.

If Europe today is at all justified in appealing to a Judeo-Christian heritage, it must not downplay anti-Semitism or ignore the Muslim actors in its history, as the saviours of the Occident are fond of doing. The religious element that was absorbed into the Enlightenment, and thus into the European project too, is found in the extension of the political space, the polis, to include *all* people, regardless of race, religion and background: *Alle Menschen werden Brüder*, says the European anthem: *all* the people shall be brothers. The nationalist concept of freedom, on the other hand, which the European project sought to transcend or at least to defuse, is necessarily limited to one's own group. The rights of others, whether immigrants or Greeks, whether the poor or oppressed of the world, are a matter of indifference at best. A global political community, to recall the beautiful phrase of the 1970s, which is merely an extrapolation of Kant's idea of eternal peace – a global political community is by definition impossible for nationalism.

At present, right-wing populism seems to be losing ground, in part because political responsibility wears it out, and in part because the massacre of Oslo has exposed its already forgotten potential for violence, which lies in the ideological exaltation of a given group's ethnic origins. But if the European Union should in fact disintegrate, or even just continue to decline, deteriorating into a purely economic community, then nationalism's dark side will also return: there can only be a group of 'us' if it is distinguished from other groups. Not only could conflicts between countries which we have long thought resolved break out within or along the borders of Europe: the pluralism that has developed within the individual nations since the end of the Second World War would be still more endangered. Those who imagined a united Europe in the nineteenth and early twentieth centuries, and those who built it out of the rubble of the Second World War, were striving for liberty, equality, solidarity. We must strive for liberty, equality, solidarity if we want to preserve, regain and expand that united Europe.

18

Triumph of Vulgar Rationalism

The Outcry over Martin Mosebach and the Ban on Circumcision

Süddeutsche Zeitung, 30 June 2012

The term courage in public debate has come to mean its opposite. Those who express resentments that most people harbour in secret, those who inveigh against migrants, people on benefits, Sinti and Roma, either Islam or the state of Israel, previously Eastern Europe, more recently the Greeks, and always against the European project; those who argue pseudo-empirically for blanket prejudices using doctored statistics, carry water for nationalists and declare whole segments of the population a menace – they not only have ideal prospects of being marketed by the country's two largest media concerns and prominently televised, although with the obligatory critical veneer, by the public networks. Those who do all of these things are assured not only of high circulation, overfilled readings, gushing royalties and the many laudatory letters that are held up with almost ritual regularity to academic detractors who study the matter in question. No, those who, as the voice of the majority, incite animosity against this or that minority do so always with the pretence of daring. In rebutting Thilo Sarrazin, who quite openly draws on ethnic-national ideology, the current president of Germany did not choose to deny his courage. But what is courageous about writing something that is sure to be rewarded with money, fame and the approval of millions?

On 18 June, the Frankfurt writer Martin Mosebach published an article in the *Frankfurter Rundschau* and the *Berliner Zeitung* on the possible criminalization of blasphemy, an article which met in published opinion with complete rejection. Many of the rebuttals extend their opprobrium to cover Mosebach's entire oeuvre, summoning negative reviews in the effort to disqualify him as an author at all. Whether left-wing intellectuals such as Ingo Schulze and Sibylle Berg, whether far-right forums such as *Politically Incorrect* and *Achgut* – all of them not only criticize Mosebach but also refuse to argue with him as a respectable author.

In the online comments under the articles, which normally offer reliable support to the putative provocateurs of political correctness, the condemnation of Mosebach can be seen to escalate rapidly into invective and regular tirades of hatred. It goes almost without saying that no approval is forthcoming from the churches when someone points up the protection of religious sensitivities. But even the conservative associations of Muslims keep silent, although the writer must have been saying exactly what they felt. Here the term 'courage' would in fact be fitting: to the public, in its religious vacuum, there seems to be hardly anything more blasphemous than questioning the right to blaspheme.

Mosebach's article, as it happens, does invite dissent. His sympathy for scandalized Muslims 'who want to give blasphemous artists – so to speak – a good scare' is hard to bear at a time when a rapper must fear for his life in Germany after Iranian ayatollahs' incitements to murder him. The idea that art would benefit, no less, from the curtailment of its freedom may be historically supported, or it may be kitsch rooted in the aesthetics of genius – in either case, inferring a wish for unfreedom would not only be politically disastrous but would degrade the aesthetic process to an act of masochism. But, most importantly, there are a number of good reasons, including religious reasons by the way, why blasphemy should not be a matter for the penal code. Christianity's history and contemporary Iran demonstrate clearly that the motivation of those who condemn others as blasphemers is very rarely spiritual and very often political.

But is Mosebach really demanding a tougher blasphemy law, as the scandalized critics say? The pertinent sentences of his article are all phrased in the subjunctive – indicating hypothesis, a thought experiment. In contrast to the picture now being painted of him as an obtuse reactionary, Mosebach is one of Germany's very few urbane contemporary authors. His descriptions of foreign cultures, particularly those little appreciated in this country, are unparalleled in their empathy and respect for the other. Mosebach is far too experienced not to know, in view of the antireligious sentiment in the society, which he laments at length, and in view of the political majorities even among Christian Democrats, that a prohibition of blasphemy in Germany is beyond all feasibility.

The actual point of his article, which remained unaddressed next to the impropriety of his objection to the defamation of faith, is to call attention to the fact that criticism of religion is devalued where religion itself tends to be seen as worthless or even harmful. After all, Martin Mosebach finds there is both moral and aesthetic justification for artists who feel compelled by a truly inner motivation, born of a serious critical engagement, to insult 'the faith of those to whom God is present'. What he objects to is 'blasphemy as a cavalier attitude or as a calculated gimmick'.

Any reader, opera-goer or theatre spectator who has shaken their head at the ignorance, the arbitrariness and, most of all, the marketing acumen with which the sacred is disparaged in the art scene can not only understand Mosebach's ire – they will also concur with it, if only for aesthetic reasons. It is no coincidence that there was a great deal of agreement on the panel of the Essen Institute for Advanced Study in the Humanities, for which Mosebach wrote his article, with the philosopher Carl Hegemann of all people: as the longstanding head of dramaturgy at the Volksbühne in Berlin, and as a colleague of Christoph Schlingensief, Hegemann was often enough involved in developing productions that were suspected of blasphemy. And perhaps I may recall at this juncture that I myself was accused three years ago of having insulted Christianity. At that time, Martin Mosebach was the first to defend me, and against a representative of his own church.

But the striking lack of understanding for anything that arises from motivations which are not secular is not just aesthetically disastrous, inasmuch as it blocks off access to broad sectors of the history of human – including Western and modern German – art and literature. The religious tone-deafness that generally goes hand in hand with an ignorance of one's own cultural tradition also raises serious problems for social cohesion, as long as some citizens or segments of the population are not indifferent to God. For what is often called indifference is anything but that and is often highly sectarian towards those who do not see the world so indifferently. The most recent example is the judgement of the Cologne regional court which has prohibited the circumcision of Jewish and Muslim children because it sees the operation as nothing but bodily harm.

Of course, if one disregards the reality of faith, tradition, the scriptures considered holy, prehistoric ritual and religious law and considers the matter purely from the standpoint of the here and now, with the logic of that sense which calls itself common, and if one at the same time ignores the history of anti-Semitism, in which the prohibition of circumcision has a central part, then one can, indeed perhaps one must, see the holy act only as bodily harm and an intolerable infringement upon the child's autonomy. If a divine commandment is nothing but hocus-pocus and every rite must be measured against the standards of the currently prevailing common sense, then a German regional court's presumption to declare four thousand years of religious history obsolete by a simple wave of a hand becomes explainable. By such logic, blasphemy too is about as bad as shouting insults at a wall. This is not the legacy of the Enlightenment. Enlightenment, as it has been taught by German philosophy in particular, would mean setting one's own worldview in perspective and taking into account, in one's own actions and words, the fact that others see the world quite differently: I may not believe in God, but I take into consideration that others do; we are unable to pass final judgement as to who is right. Enlightenment is not simply the rule of reason but at the same time the realization that reason is limited.

Vulgar rationalism, on the other hand, as expressed in the judgement of the Cologne regional court, posits its own understanding, today's understanding, as absolute. From there it is not far to biologism, which applies a purely scientific view of Creation to the study of society. It is conspicuous that the right-wing forums which rage against Martin Mosebach are also the most vehement in their support for Thilo Sarrazin. And those intellectuals on the left who are taking a public stance against their colleague are also not known to have objected so promptly to Sarrazin's anti-immigration manifesto *Deutschland schafft sich ab* [Germany abolishes itself]. Admittedly, it would have taken courage to oppose the media conglomerates on which we as authors are dependent.

19

Too Late for Good Conscience

The Civil War in Syria

Süddeutsche Zeitung, 28 June 2013

Thundering is the silence with which people of the word, the scholars and the men and women of letters worldwide, react to the war in Syria. The maelstrom of brutality, destitution, expulsion and denominational schism in which the Syrians' uprising has been caught up is no longer mentioned except in foreign policy reporting. It's enough to drive a person mad: with significant involvement of foreign states, a conflict escalates which could unleash a deluge of violence, terrorism, mass migration, lawlessness and ethnic or denominational cleansing not only upon a country, a society of rare diversity, and magnificent relics of ancient civilization but on the whole strategically vital region – and the chronically overheating talk machine of our literary life devotes not even a panel discussion to the disaster.

And yet the danger is no longer merely that of another Lebanon or Afghanistan – that is, a civil war between parties which are more or less defined and which only need to exhaust their strength before swinging back into a peace process. The danger in Syria – as the special envoy of the United Nations, Lakhdar Brahimi, prophesied – is a deterioration like Somalia's. Except that the nightmare of a permanently lawless zone teeming with weapons, mafia-like cartels, state-aligned death squads and religious extremists will not play out on the remote margins of global attention and interests, where at most a few warships would need to be sent to protect passing merchant shipping from pirates. No, this nightmare is already happening now in the immediate vicinity of Europe, Israel and several Arab states that are wobbly enough as it is. Those who are not interested in the fate of the Syrians should take a glance at a map if they want to look out for their own security and stability.

Yes, the conflict has grown complicated. Although there were ways, in the beginning, to support the democratic opposition, there was no will in the West to undertake a serious engagement in the Syrian conflict; but now that there is a will in some capitals, the ways are no longer available. As many predicted, there are now more and more holy warriors, many of them from abroad, mixed in with the insurgents, so that supplying machine guns and bulletproof vests will not balance out the mismatched arsenals but would at best – or at worst? – make the war drag on longer. The government troops have scored too many victories recently, and the jihadists among the civilian population have spread too much terror, for the regime to go on fearing it could collapse under mass desertions. Furthermore, as the rebels grow more radical and at the same time more fragmented, their willingness and indeed their competence to accept a compromise – an agreement with representatives of the state that will ultimately be necessary – declines. A population that stood up to repression for many weeks of truly heroic mass protest in 2011, peacefully, creatively and resolutely secularly for that matter, is being ground down on the battlefield – and punished for desiring freedom by seeing its cities devastated.

What can be done? The reader will not expect a conclusive answer, I hope. There are no good options any more that can be advocated in good conscience. It is too late for good conscience. No matter what the West could still do now to influence developments in Syria – it will be insufficient and entail heavy risks. But among all the bad options, the one Europe has chosen once again – doing nothing – is almost the most dangerous. Because doing nothing means standing by while others do something. While Russia, Iran and Hisbollah keep the dictatorship alive, Saudi Arabia and Qatar are doing their best to fan the denominational war between Sunnis and Shiites.

Only democracy is not backed by any foreign power. Worse still, the support that the radical Islamists receive from the Gulf states is naturally perceived by the Syrians as Western support. After all, the West has no closer allies in the region than Saudi Arabia and Qatar. And the criticism of Assad's sponsors would be a good deal more credible – and a peace conference a good deal more likely – if the West would finally challenge the jihadists' sponsors too. But that is apparently not possible for strategic reasons. Because in fact the old East–West conflict is having a new run in the Middle East as a schism between Shia and Sunna. The interchangeability of the ideological motives is underscored by the fact that the Iranian theocracy, of all parties, is joining Russia as a protector of the secular Assad regime while America pins its hopes on the Islamist forces, not only in Syria but also in Egypt and other countries of the Arab Spring.

What Syria needs is not more weapons, but fewer. Instead of joining in the arms build-up, the West should throw its weight behind stopping military aid and getting the foreign powers to make their proxies commit to a ceasefire. The threat of supplying arms can generate pressure to bring about disarmament, as political experience teaches us and as Russia's relenting, accepting at least the demand for a transitional government, now shows. Threats only work, however, if they can be carried out: this is one of the inadequacies and grave risks that any policy towards Syria brings with it today.

The rebellion has not yet turned into an outright civil war which would pit the Sunni majority on one side against the Alawites, supported by the other minorities, such as the Christians and Druze, on the other. The fact that the two most important opposition groups are led by Christians, Georges Sabra and Georges Kilo, is itself evidence that the divisions are not yet strictly along denominational boundaries. It is also true, however, that extremists on both sides of the front are inflaming religious hatred. The regime derives its legitimacy from the radicalism of its opponents, which it therefore stokes systematically, for example by deploying Alawite militias specifically to massacre Sunni villagers. Conversely, the jihadists intentionally attack members of the religious minorities so that the rebellion will finally degenerate into the war of religion which is their *raison d'être*. The extremely fragile situation of the Christians, who are not at all as unanimously in the government camp as many claim, is exacerbated by the fact that the Syrian churches are not neutral but have been siding with Assad since the beginning of the protests, maintaining a deathly silence, in the true sense of the word, about the massacres and air strikes.

Of all the cities of the Middle East, Damascus and Aleppo were perhaps the most shining examples – enchanting every visitor – of the possibility of a peaceful coexistence among different ethnicities, languages and religions. Europe, which all but extinguished its original diversity in the twentieth century with concentration camps and ethnic purges, cannot pretend to be a schoolmaster of tolerance. But it could, with its experience, help to prevent other societies from taking a similar wrong turn. Who if not the people of the word has a duty to remind Europe of the responsibility it bears, including a responsibility for Syria?

20

Farewell to the Middle East

The 'Islamic State's' March on Baghdad

Die Zeit, 26 June 2014

For a quarter of a century, more than half my lifetime, I have been travelling in the Middle East, and besides Isfahan I have lived in Cairo and Beirut. Not once have I ever had any difficulty, been insulted, avoided, or looked at askance because of my belonging to Shia Islam, which Sunnis readily deduce from my Iranian background. Occasionally a villager or a tradesman asks whether Shiites recognize Muhammad as the Prophet, or whether it's true that they revere his son-in-law, Imam Ali, as God – that does happen. But it was never in a hostile, aggressive tone; in the countryside especially it was more the amazement of meeting a real live Shiite face to face, one evidently kindly disposed towards them as Sunnis, or at least interested in them, and one whose faith is not essentially different from theirs: Please sit down and have tea.

I fell in love with the Arab world altogether in 1989 when I first backpacked through Syria, in part because it appeared to me far more tolerant, more hospitable, towards the stranger, towards the other, towards even the oddest birds, than Europe, than Germany at the time in particular, which seemed never to have heard of integration in spite of millions of immigrants. In the provinces, where I grew up – happily, I hasten to state; I hardly ever felt discriminated against – I was the only one for miles around who didn't look like everyone else, and an ordinary German pub was like a forbidding fortress to me, repellently homogeneous down to the oak interior and the stags' antlers.

Every Arab tea house, on the other hand, looked to me like a glorious melting pot: the never-matching furnishings representing every corner of the earth and every century; to say nothing of the guests, who belonged to so many different classes, ethnicities, religions, sexual orientations – although they all lived in the same neighbourhood. Even if it wasn't so important to me personally, I was happy to set out my Iranian background, my German birthplace, my Shiite religion and even my Cologne football loyalty, if only to contribute a few exotic splotches to the many colours present. Reliably, the locals bought me my next tea.

This is beginning to sound like a fairy tale, I realize. And, yes, as a young student of course I had a one-sided, freshly infatuated view of the Arab world, idealizing the gaps and the contradictions, romanticizing the already rampant poverty as simplicity; I did not ignore the political dictatorship, especially in Syria, but I was intoxicated with the romance of true resistance and actually believed I was playing hide-and-seek with the ubiquitous secret police. Yet I was not the only one; the German friends with whom I travelled in the Arab countries and studied in Egypt, Annette and Henriette, Michi and Andreas, felt no less like fish in water when we prowled the old quarters at night, stumbling from a gay bar to a spiritual dance ritual; getting invited here to prayers, there to a glass of hard liquor, and sometimes to the liquor after the prayers; hearing the muezzin competing at dawn with the dance music and, in bed at last, being woken up by church bells. If there was one thing we loved about the Arabs because it wasn't familiar to us from Germany, it was their talent for letting what was different be different: not having to resolve contradictions, not having to question all the questionable things, not needing to investigate the sounds and smells that waft into the room from next door. It is exactly what stands out so in Arab cultural history: Islamic Studies has no explanation for the regularity with which Islam is violated within Islam.

The most famous poet of Arabic literary history, often quoted by classical theologians, is Abu Nuwas, whose poems celebrate not only wine but also homosexuality and even Satan himself, and the *Thousand and One Nights* are peppered with at least as many sex scenes as Quran verses. An orthodox Quran commentator always offers different and mutually contradictory interpretations of a verse, to conclude invariably that God knows best, and that also says something about a culture that sees the unambiguous, the overly exact definition, as hubris, human presumption, thus almost an abomination. That world that we as students were able to discover no longer exists. It became a fairy tale definitively when the 'Islamic State in Iraq and Syria' (ISIS) advanced on Baghdad, where once Harun al-Rashid and Scheherazade had lived, and where up to the end of the 1940s Jews had still been the largest and the intellectually leading ethnic group.

What has happened? When I try to set out clearly what led to the fratricidal war that threatens to tear the Middle East apart, I – no, I do not have to go back to the year 680, when the caliph's army massacred Imam Hussein and seventy-two of his companions at Karbala, in what is now Iraq. Nor do I have to refer to colonial dominance, whose methods included playing one segment of the population against another; other foreign rulers did so too before the British and the Russians came. A more important date is 16 January 1979, when a Shiite revolution drove the shah of Iran out of the country. The United States, having thus lost its most important partner in the region, responded by arming Iran's Arab and hence Sunni neighbours: first the Iraqi dictator Saddam Hussein, who attacked Iran somewhat more than a year after the revolution; and subsequently the monarchies across the Persian Gulf, whose Wahhabi ideology ranks the Shiites as more contemptible than ordinary unbelievers. Thus, to contain Shiite fundamentalism, Washington made a pact with its Sunni counterpart. While the Iranians miserably failed to export their revolution, the Wahhabis were able to expand their influence to the edges of the Muslim world, as far as Central Asia in the East and Bosnia in the West.

As early as the late 1980s, we saw the first zealots on the streets of Cairo: the men with ankle-length jellabiyas, white caps on their shorn heads and chest-length beards; the women with the still unfamiliar niqab, somehow shocking when you first see it face to face, leaving nothing of the body visible except a slit for the eyes. People called them Wahhabis, or simply Saudis, because they seemed as exotic as visitors from Mars, simply by their appearance and by their laboured high-Arabic, old-fashioned way of speaking. But they were just a few individuals, and when I talked to them I sometimes made the acquaintance of young men and not at all shy women, almost all of whom were active in society and had taken up their uniform, so it seemed to me at any rate, out of a rebelliousness that was not so fundamentally different from that of Western youth movements. They would eventually abandon their uniforms like a passing fashion, we hoped at the time.

What we experienced as more threatening was that almost none of our Arab friends had any prospect of ever starting a family. Even if they were able to find a steady job – as a teacher, as a clerk or even in a government agency, which was improbable enough – they still wouldn't be able to afford a flat of their own; the only way to do that was to get married. It was obvious to everyone that this lack of prospects would someday boil over: the psychological pressures of living with their parents, along with three, four likewise grown-up siblings; sexual frustration not least among them because the increasingly crowded conditions on the outskirts of the cities no longer offered the niches of freedom found in the traditional city centres. Only no one knew when the lid would blow off and whether the explosion would be a violent one. The old, beautiful *fin-de-siècle* buildings in the inner cities decayed; the public spaces fell into neglect. As the standards in the hopelessly overcrowded and underfinanced educational institutions declined dramatically, the intellectual discourse also atrophied. Or was it the other way around? As early as 1989, the older inhabitants rhapsodized about bygone days, about Beirut in the sixties, Cairo in the fifties and Baghdad in the forties, the way we rhapsodize today about the Arab world of our student years.

In the years that followed, the first terrorist attacks in Egypt jolted us awake. And yet we thought then that the violence itself signalled the decline of political Islam. By striking the nerve centre of the economy, the centres of tourism (and at the same time the core of their own culture, hospitality), the terrorists lost their support among the population. Hideouts were betrayed, funding channels boycotted; the police rapidly broke up the terror groups' whole structure. In spite of the widespread poverty, the corrupt rulers and the despotism, the violent groups were nowhere able to win over the majority or even just a significant proportion of the destitute, despairing youth.

Everywhere in the Muslim world, political Islam was tending towards the centre, was gentrifying, renouncing violence and conquering the institutions: in Turkey with Erbakan and later with Erdoğan, in Iran with President Khatami and the reform movement, in Indonesia with the big, moderate Islamic parties and their reform agendas, in Jordan and Morocco with the Islamists in coalition governments; in a different and portentous way in Egypt, where a puritanical, mindless and humourless piety flooded the entire public discourse to arm the state against the Islamists, whose activists were rotting in the prisons at the time. Persecuted by the security services, isolated from the population, frustrated by their strategy's lack of success, the leaders of the terrorist groups found refuge, after a few detours, in Afghanistan, which had been overrun by the Taliban with Saudi, Pakistani and American help. The massacres that the Taliban were committing there against thousands of Shiite Hazaras had not yet come to the attention of the global public. The rest of the story is all the more well known since 11 September 2001.

This form of political violence was new not only to America. Until then, the Arab terrorists had attacked their own governments. In the Twin Towers, however, they spectacularly destroyed the symbol of a civilization, a way of life. The ideology of jihadism was born: its thinking, complementary to that of globalization, is no longer in national categories but declares the whole world the battlefield of a war between faith and unbelief. What makes the actors of this ideology so dangerous is that they are themselves children of globalization, from the businessman bin Laden, who attended the same school in Beirut as Omar Sharif, to the upper-class Egyptian doctor al-Zawahiri; from the FC St Pauli fan Mohamed Atta to the German converts returning from Syria: they know exactly how to cause their enemy the greatest terror because the enemy is their own past, their own secular socialization. The videos of beheaded prisoners that are now being placed online again from the conquered areas in Iraq are not simply barbaric – they are meant to be barbaric; that is, we are dealing not with savages but with people who are coolly and strategically acting like savages.

No one knows what would have happened to jihadism if the United States hadn't launched the Iraq War. But what we do know is that the war has horribly fulfilled the predictions of those who argued against it. After losing its camps and its sources of funding in Afghanistan, jihadism has received the gift of a gigantic, strategically much better located, financially lucrative staging area in the centre of the Arab world, near to Europe and nearer still to Israel – and, as a free bonus, new reasons to hate the West in the form of Abu Ghraib and the American oil deals. The conflagration that so many political leaders and practically all the experts warned against is taking place right now. Judging by the chaos and the millions of victims, intended and unintended, for which they are responsible, there would be justice in global politics only if George W. Bush and Dick Cheney, Paul Wolfowitz and Tony Blair spent the rest of their lives behind bars. They say there are a few vacancies, at last, in Guantánamo Bay.

But to return to history, which took a turn that surprised us all ten years after 9/11: the revolution. Like Baron Munchhausen, the Arabs and especially the hopeless youth, who had always looked to me as though they had been left behind, now seemed to be pulling themselves out of the bog by their own bootstraps. The social and psychological pressure that had been obvious twenty-five years earlier had boiled over in Cairo and Tunis, in Manama and Sanaa, as a peaceful, undogmatic, multi-class, multi-denominational, multi-generational and multi-gendered rebellion. And, as great as the disappointments of the subsequent years have been, the last word on the Arab Spring has not yet been spoken: revolutions cannot be settled up after three but, rather, after thirty years. At any rate, structures that once seemed to have been ordained by God have been proved once for all to be changeable, and Islamism, wherever it was elected to public office, discredited itself surprisingly quickly. Some countries, most probably Tunisia and, after a dictatorial interregnum, perhaps Egypt too, may still make it the rest of the way from liberation to freedom; others, however, have already toppled into the abyss.

In the West German provinces where I grew up, there had been only Germans and only churches since the Second World War. As I said, I am not writing this because I felt discriminated against. I only want to explain why I was so amazed when I backpacked around Syria in 1989. There were Arabs, Alawites, Druze, Kurds, Circassians, Turks, Armenians, Assyrians and Jews; in every city there were mosques and churches, and in Damascus centuries-old synagogues. I don't want to idealize the Syria of that time, which was a horrible political dictatorship, but everyone who knows the region will agree that the coexistence of so many ethnicities, languages and religions worked better, and the various minorities enjoyed more respect and more rights, than in the rest of the Arab world.

How tragic that the pursuit of freedom has unintentionally unleashed sectarianism. In 2012, when I was reporting on the war in Syria, I no longer chose to display my Shiite denomination in Sunni areas, and my Sunni driver broke out in a sweat whenever we approached a checkpoint of the Alawite Shabiha militias. If we were travelling in the countryside, where we might meet both government troops and insurgents, he always had a cross hanging from his rear-view mirror to signal neutrality. Two years later, I wouldn't dare enter the rebel-held areas as a Shiite, and my Sunni driver would not drive cross-country even with a cross on his mirror.

The people who had peacefully marched in the streets for democracy were no doubt aware of the fragility of their very diverse society. Precisely because the Assad regime was identified with a certain ethnic group, the Alawites, the demonstrators all over Syria were careful to phrase their protest without any indication of specific religions or ethnicities. In vain: the regime repeatedly sent purely Alawite militias into Sunni villages and let its bombs rain specifically on Sunni neighbourhoods to turn the uprising for freedom into a war of religion. The strategy behind the massacres was clear, and it worked: Assad stoked the hatred of the Sunni suburban and rural population, rallying the minorities and the urban middle and upper classes, who had good reason to fear Islamic fundamentalism. While the peaceful demonstrators and the secular Free Army hoped in vain for Western support, or at least a no-fly zone, Saudi Arabia and Qatar for their part armed the jihadists infiltrating Syria. The country became the setting for a proxy war between Iran and the Gulf states, which in turn were allied with Russia and America respectively. Thus the old East–West conflict was revived in the Middle East along the boundaries between Sunnis and Shiites. Only an understanding between Iran and the United States, whose falling-out had set the spiral of sectarian violence in motion, could still pacify the region – assuming it is not far too late now for peace.

As in the Thirty Years' War, which began with a denominational schism but took on a life of its own as a struggle for power, money and influence between individual warlords in shifting alliances, the motives of the militias and their sponsors in the new Middle East are hard to penetrate. While the Iranian theocracy stands behind the secularist Assad regime, the secular West supports Sunni fundamentalism through its alliance with Saudi Arabia. Meanwhile, Damascus itself let the ISIS leaders out of prison at the beginning of the uprising. As if by chance, jihadist groups infiltrated into Syria from Iraq at the same time; they did not attack government-controlled positions but seized power in the areas that had already been conquered by the Free Army and other opposition groups. As we know today, Assad even bought oil from ISIS to finance the most extreme faction of the opponents facing him.

Anyway the jihadists would be stupid – which they obviously are not – to attack Damascus with the few thousand fighters they have, who include numerous mercenaries, deserters, criminals and converts from Europe with little combat experience, and, if I am not mistaken yet again, they will not attack Baghdad either, and least of all the south of Iraq, where they would have to expect the resistance of the Shiite population. Conversely, Iraq's Shiite head of government Maliki has not said a word to indicate any intention to retake the cities lost. As in Syria, ISIS will first consolidate its rule in the Sunni territories that have been left to fend for themselves by the central government. Except that those are not, strictly speaking, Sunni territories. Up until recently, the west and north of Iraq, as in Syria, were inhabited by people of diverse ethnic backgrounds and religions living side by side. The homogeneous neighbourhoods and cities, and soon provinces, date only from the Iraq War, which bestowed power on a practically pure Shiite government. Like Germany after the Thirty Years' War and Europe after the Second World War, the future Middle East will also be largely divided into denominationally and ethnically homogeneous territories. Whether it will still be worth while stopping in the tea houses then, I don't know.

21

STOP THE 'ISLAMIC STATE'!

The Threat of Genocide against Christians, Yazidis and other Ethnic Groups in Iraq

Frankfurter Rundschau, Berliner Zeitung, Kölner Stadtanzeiger, Mitteldeutsche Zeitung, 15 August 2014

A civilizational consensus seems to be jelling that the world community – no, not just the Americans – must prevent the impending genocide of Christians, Yazidis and other religious minorities. Both the American and Iranian governments are supplying weapons to the Kurds who are resisting the 'Islamic State' (IS); the arch-enemies are also jointly supporting the designated prime minister Haider al-Abadi in his attempt to finally form an interdenominational government in Baghdad. European foreign policy has surprisingly easily slipped the fetters of its notorious divisions by declaring itself irrelevant and giving the national governments free rein to intervene or not, or to intervene just a little bit. In Germany, such fundamentally different politicians as Gregor Gysi, Cem Özdemir and Elmar Brok agree that the opponents of the 'Islamic State' need military support – from Germany. And the Greens, who came into existence with the peace movement, were the first party explicitly to approve of the American air strikes against IS positions – and with the remarkably self-reflective observation that terrorists can be defeated not on yoga mats and in discussion groups but 'the way the Americans do it'. There are reasons to hope that the world community will yet intervene in time to establish humanitarian corridors for the refugees and to prevent the fall of Kurdish cities such as Erbil which have become havens for the persecuted minorities. But will that be enough?

No, it can only be the beginning. American air strikes and weapons for the Kurds will be able to slow the IS offensive, and perhaps stop it – but they will not liberate a metropolis such as Mosul. Neither the future government of Iraq nor the world community must tolerate a terror group of twenty thousand, according to generous estimates, which rules a territory the size of Germany, subjecting it to brutal ethnic and religious purges and tyrannizing the remaining indigenous population, and which will soon invade the Sunni areas in northern Lebanon, with greater chances of permanent presence there than in Kurdistan, and capture another major city, Tripoli. Then a Pol Pot version of Islam would rule from the Iranian border to the Mediterranean Sea.

Europe could, indeed must perhaps, accept that the national borders in the Middle East will be demolished – after all, they were drawn so arbitrarily in the twentieth century that a rearrangement would not necessarily worsen them. What is not acceptable to any empathetic heart is for a single terror group such as IS to destroy the fragile and yet so valuable, so culturally rich fabric of very different ethnicities, religions and languages that has developed with relative continuity over many thousands of years in the eastern Mediterranean. The fight against such an extremism claiming a justification in Islam must not be carried on by America alone, nor by Christian countries concerned – rightly – about their co-religionists. This fight must also be the fight of the Islamic countries, and not just that of their governments, but their theologians, their intellectuals, the

Muslim peoples as a whole. It is their own traditions that the jihadists are declaring obsolete in favour of an imaginary prehistory that is historically, dogmatically and, most of all, humanly indefensible.

No other world religion owes more to direct communication with the theologians, translators, philosophers, literary scholars and scientists of other religions and peoples than Islam, which in its formative period was far from being the majority religion in the Middle East. Its intellectual and cultural flowering was never only its own but also the flowering of other, older traditions, which Islam in its prime absorbed instead of outlawing them. The Arab world especially has never been able to compensate culturally for the exodus of its Jews after the founding of the state of Israel. If now the remaining minorities, first among them the Christians, should disappear or persist only in limited enclaves, Middle Eastern civilization will be as withered as the desert out of which its prophets came. What is now impending, or already happening, in these days in the summer of 2014 is comparable in its dimensions and its effects on the Middle East only with the dimensions and effects of the First World War in Europe – not excluding the still greater and more disastrous war that followed it. For Europe too, which for all its upgraded border security will not be able to insulate itself from its immediate neighbours, the consequences would also be tangible: for every single citizen; for their prosperity, their safety, their tolerance; for the coexistence of the different ethnicities and cultures in European cities.

What then can be done? Those who claim to know the exact answer already are not being honest. The situation is so complicated, the individual conflicts have so long been intertwined, the fronts so interlocked and the past mistakes so huge – mistakes that can no longer be undone, and not only those of American Middle East policy – that we would have to begin, alongside humanitarian aid and the unavoidable current military mission, by untangling the various threads that have become knotted up in a calamity of biblical proportions. The mention of a CSCE by Foreign Minister Frank-Walter Steinmeier is itself an indication of the only scale on which the Middle East might yet be pacified. Iraq and, still more, Syria must first become states again in the full sense of the term: they must provide the basic necessities throughout the country, show at least the rudiments of the rule of law and, not least, include all denominations and ethnicities in their armed forces in order to resist fanatical marauders, many of them entering from abroad, pretending to be the avengers of a given oppressed ethnic group.

We won't defeat terrorists with rolled yoga mats under our arms. But if at least those countries that are directly involved in the conflicts would consider their common interest in stability, there would indeed be something they could do against twenty thousand fighters, merciless as they may be: the United States, with its disastrous invasion of Iraq and its equally mistaken premature withdrawal; Iran with its Shiite clientele politics which have driven the Sunni population into the extremists' camp; the Gulf states with their billions in support of jihadist groups; Turkey, which kept its southeastern border open to the 'Islamic State' all too long; Syria, which is waging a war against the majority of its own population; Russia, which stands, along with Iran, behind the inhuman Assad regime; and, finally, Europe, which is unable to make sensible use of its enormous economic, political and diplomatic potential on the world stage.

The moment has now come when even the most obdurate government should realize that the monster created in the Great Game of the early twenty-first century threatens its interests too. The game must stop: stop the 'Islamic State'!

22

The European Ideal is Sinking

The Mediterranean Sea as a Mass Grave

Frankfurter Allgemeine Zeitung, 22 April 2015

In the autumn of 2005 I visited the Spanish enclave of Ceuta on the Moroccan coast. During the previous night, hundreds of refugees had tried to get past the border fortifications, which at that time were already reminiscent of the pre-1990 German–German border and have since been further reinforced: two barbed-wire fences, 3 and 6 metres high; between them a road patrolled by Guardia Civil jeeps; watchtowers of course; video cameras, infrared binoculars. If five hundred people at once storm the border fence with home-made ladders, fifty will get through – that was the strategy. A few bleed to death each time, at each of these assaults; the rest are trucked into the desert between Morocco and Algeria, where they are driven from the open truck bed like animals – with a few water canisters in the best case, in the middle of literally nothing.

I didn't go directly to the official border station, where I would immediately have been waved through with my German passport. I went to the fence and saw something that made a more lasting impression on me than all the news of refugee disasters in the Mediterranean Sea since then, with two hundred or four hundred or six hundred dead. Those are just numbers; we don't see the people who have drowned; we don't know their stories. That is why we forget those numbers so quickly, and with them the European Union's promises to try to prevent such disasters in the future. But now I have seen the blood on Europe's borders, the blood that goes on dripping today.

We still vaguely remember the advertising poster of the fashion label Benetton with the hopelessly overcrowded ship at Bari, the nine hundred and eleven refugees who landed on the beach at Boulouris, and the ghost ship that was towed to the coast of Lampedusa, all its passengers having drowned. Fifteen years ago, those scenes made headlines similar to those of this week about the capsizing of the hopelessly overloaded fishing boat 130 kilometres off the Libyan coast, which resulted, by current estimates, in some nine hundred refugees drowning. Since then, the announcements have always been the same: fight people-smugglers; expand marine search and rescue; fight the causes of migration; unify European asylum law. What has been accomplished is: the opposite. In fact, the numbers of victims grow from year to year, and experts assume by now that several tens of thousands of refugees have drowned in the Mediterranean Sea in recent years. Our holiday beaches look out on a mass grave.

People-smugglers? Yes, most of them are ruthless criminals, if not murderers, and they need to be brought to justice – but they will continue to exist as long as people have no legal way to flee destitution, oppression and death.

Search and rescue? By founding the so-called Frontex agency, the European Union has ensured that the refugee boats must take progressively longer, more dangerous routes in order to dodge the European warships. The 12 kilometres that separate Spain and Morocco at the narrowest point are often extended to an odyssey of several hundred kilometres.

The only programme that effectively saved lives was the Italian operation Mare Nostrum, which was criticized by Germany the loudest and was abandoned after a year for lack of EU funding.

Causes of migration? Europe is not responsible for all the misery in the world, and I am not listing here the EU subsidies that are destroying Africa's cotton and sugar industries, nor the tariffs we use to exclude African products from the market, nor climate change, which, according to United Nations predictions, will have made two-thirds of Africa's farmland into desert by 2025. The chief cause of the current rise in refugee numbers is the deterioration of governance in the countries of North Africa and the Middle East. Europe has not slowed that deterioration but in fact advanced it by supporting ruthless despots for decades, even in the middle of the Arab rebellions. The word 'Euro-Mediterranean Process', which sounds like an EU programme to save sidewalk cafés or to swap southern cooking recipes, actually means closer collaboration with these dictators in order to protect Europe from refugees and terrorists, as we read in the strategy papers of the EU think tanks: 'refugees and terrorists', in the same European breath.

The civil wars and anarchic conditions in many Arab countries today cannot be understood without the tyrannies that preceded them, which left behind dysfunctional societies, disaffiliated middle classes, appalling poverty, dilapidated educational systems and religious fanaticism. The Iraq War, which was waged against the resistance of some European countries, it is true, but from European airfields (and with the express permission of the present chancellor, Angela Merkel), has created a failed state in the immediate vicinity of Europe which could soon be overrun by Quran-toting mass murderers. When peaceful demonstrators in Syria took to the streets to demand democracy, Europe looked on passively as the Assad regime crossed one red line after another, until the country finally sank into the predictable civil war.

But the most devastating thing, morally and strategically, is the alliance that the West, and thus Europe too, has entered into with the primary sponsor of militant Islamism, Saudi Arabia. After all, the 'Islamic State' distributes in every city it conquers, from day one, the writings of the Saudi preacher Ibn Abd al-Wahhab. The hundreds of thousands of Arab Christians who have had to flee Iraq and Syria are not the only immediate victims of this ideology of hatred that has been and continues to be propagated to the entire Islamic world from Saudi Arabia. If we wonder why the alliance with a radical fundamentalist and dictatorial state is the central pillar of Western and European Middle East policy, we need look no further than the lowered price of oil that has reliably restarted our economy in times of crisis. The Saudis are no ingrates, at least.

Of course, other countries are also responsible for the mass deaths in the Mediterranean Sea. But I happen to be a German writer and a European citizen addressing a German and a European public. So I speak of the German and European share in the responsibility, without overlooking the fact that Russia, for example, or Iran, Turkey or the Arab League have also contributed, and perhaps more, to the Syrian, Iraqi, Libyan and other disasters.

Oh – and the uniform European refugee policy, which at least supplied Germany with the pretext for abandoning its original fundamental right, the right to asylum, in the 1993 constitutional amendment? There is no such uniformity, and there certainly will not be in future to judge by the decline of the European idea in the EU. The member countries of the European Union are unanimous only in this: that there is no point on the outer borders of Europe where asylum can be applied for. As long as the gates of Europe are not open at least to victims of persecution, and we lock out even those we urgently need for our own economy, the blood will go on dripping.

Since I stood at the border fence in Ceuta in 2005, I have reported on the refugees, given lectures, and advocated in my home town for more humanitarian policies, as countless of my fellow citizens have done. I have also spoken with many politicians. No, they did not strike me as devoid of souls. Those whom I met seemed not only to know but to feel in their hearts that Europe is committing one of the great crimes of our time on the Mediterranean Sea today. But if I then ask why Europe, although it makes many announcements, changes nothing, I always get one answer: more refugees would drive still more people to support the far right. Then Le Pen in France would win not 25 but 40 per cent of the voters, and Pegida in Dresden would mobilize not twenty-five thousand but a hundred thousand demonstrators.

To be honest, I couldn't rebut that argument. But now, looking back over the past ten years, something has changed after all: public awareness. Speaking for Cologne, I can say this: wherever a refugee shelter is opened, a local citizens' action group immediately forms – not against, but for the refugees! I hear similar things from other cities. It is true that the anti-immigration people have gained supporters and, most of all, attention. But much more numerous are those who can no longer stand to see refugees drowning, dying of thirst or bleeding to death, being imprisoned, beaten or degraded just because they have claimed their human right to a life in dignity. Yes, I believe that by now the politicians are no longer right, and that a majority of the population would indeed be willing to do without some measure of prosperity – to pay a solidarity surtax, let's say, as we gladly did to finance German unification – to save the refugees and, with them, the European idea. But then we must also take to the streets when Pegida marches again, a million in opposition to their tens of thousands. The refugees need Europe, and now Europe needs us.

23

AT OUR CHILDREN'S COST
Europe after Brexit
Frankfurter Allgemeine Zeitung, 29 June 2016

Those born after the war in West Germany have always lived with Europe. They have never known anything else but the fault-finding with the institutions that have given political form to the project of the Enlightenment: the Coal and Steel Community, the Court of Human Rights, the European Parliament, the Brussels bureaucracy. But, through it all, Europe has been a reality; it not only existed but it continually grew stronger and larger. Yes, even the *Ach!* over Europe has been a part of that continuity.

Just a year ago, during the debt crisis and before the refugee crisis, the idea that Europe might fail was no more than a fantasy of certain somehow unappetizing parties – 'Europe' here not in the geographical sense, although, what with the nuclear threat, its sheer physical perpetuity has not always and everywhere seemed secure; but 'Europe' as a voluntary community and a political union, Europe with its inviolable fundamental rights, open borders, supranational institutions, common market and, most importantly, a judiciary that is above national law. But, since last Friday, I am not the only one with creeping misgivings that our generation of forty-, fifty-, sixty-year-olds may be bargaining away the great, yes, the historically almost unbelievable gift of European unity and bequeathing to our children a continent on which nationalism has been resurrected.

Of course, Europe's politicians comfort us and bolster our confidence; after all, that's their job. But they too will be unable to ignore the deep-seated crisis of legitimacy which has been brought upon Europe by the British referendum. Because now it is no longer just a vague impression: a European country has now demonstrated that the majority of its voters reject Europe in its present form. Of course, other nations are traditionally more supportive of Europe, but can we be sure that a referendum in France, in Germany, in Italy would not lead to the same result? And, as long as the people are not asked, the strongest argument – and perhaps an apposite one – of the opponents of Europe will be the European Union's lack of democratic legitimacy. In fact, Europe has almost always lost at the ballot box, whether in the referendums on the constitution, the Swiss referendums on EU membership or, most recently, the referendum in the Netherlands on the Association Agreement with Ukraine.

Prescient politicians may ignore polls, of course – neither the German constitution nor the Treaty of Rome nor Willy Brand's genuflection in Warsaw would have carried a referendum at the time. The Federal Republic of Germany in particular owes its present democratic foundations, its economic prosperity and its political unity to statesmen who defied the zeitgeist, such as Theodor Heuss, Konrad Adenauer, Willy Brandt and Helmut Kohl. But if their visions had not won majority approval after the fact through wise, pragmatic application, neither the country's integration in the West nor its reconciliation with Europe would have lasted long.

Europe has not been able to do likewise since it set itself the goal of political union. To find the reasons, we must go back to the beginnings of this transition: the failure of the constitution, which had not been promoted, not been championed, not been explained, and whose rejection was so passively accepted by many European heads of government as to leave the impression that they were not even sad about the results of the referendums – after all, a functioning union would have finally taken away their veto.

By devaluing the constitution to a mere treaty and abandoning its essential political provisions, the European Union has settled for structures that are not commensurate with its size and diversity. In other words, the economic process of unification was not accompanied by a political one, nor has the enlargement of the union been accompanied by a consolidation. The top positions in the European Union were at first consciously given to second- and third-tier politicians – Lady Ashton et al. – to ensure they would not interfere in the affairs of the national leaders. Even today, the important decisions are reserved to the European Council, whose members make policy for the entire continent but have to win only their national elections.

As things are organized under the Treaty of Lisbon, the EU has not been and will not be able to arrive at a consistent foreign policy, a logical security architecture, or a market with not only common buyers but also common rules and social standards, a plausible agricultural policy and sensible subsidies. Instead, the crises caused by Europe's weakening have been and are still being used as arguments, and even purposely exacerbated, to weaken Europe further – the refugee crisis is not the first time the EU has been caught in this vicious circle. Germany too first discovered its interest in a refugee policy based on solidarity when it had to bear the burdens itself. And because a circle of twenty-eight heads of government can approve general petitions but is not capable of serious action under the requirement of unanimity, the critical decisions on the fates of over five hundred million people are taken not in the competent institutions, elected or not, but almost always in bilateral preliminary talks between a few heads of government. The lack of confidence is therefore unsurprising, and Germany is accused of wielding a predominance of power not because it is so unpopular – on the contrary! – but because the Greeks, for example, were forced to observe during the debt crisis that their fate was controlled by a government which had been elected in Germany – no wonder there were outbreaks of nationalist sentiment on both the left and the right of the political spectrum.

And when practically the only argument advanced in favour of Europe is that of economic advantage, as in David Cameron's campaign, many people object that they simply do not notice that advantage in their day-to-day lives – perhaps in London or Frankfurt, but not in the Midlands or in Mecklenburg and Western Pomerania, and least of all in the south of Europe, where youth unemployment is often over 50 per cent. It does not help to do sums to show the redundant industrial workers or the pensioners how much poorer they would be without the EU. The redundant industrial worker and the pensioner would sooner believe promises of salvation through a return to the nation-state. Accordingly, the referendum in the United Kingdom was called a choice between the heart and the mind – with Europe linked to the rational mind, and thus to thinking in categories of utility. But those who reduce Europe to economic advantage will be empty-handed if the accounts do not balance.

The text of the constitution was initiated and drafted by a generation which had physically suffered through the depths of nationalism or, in the case of the veterans of '68, had been politically socialized in the aftermath of the Second World War. However, the constitutional process was carried out, publicly commented upon and thwarted through apathy by my generation, who have no biographical experience of the necessity of Europe: they appreciate, for the most part, the advantages of Brussels, they see the advantage of a common course of action in the globalized world, but their relationship to Europe is an instrumental one. During the financial crisis, too, the argumentation of Europe's politicians was purely utilitarian, as the German chancellor memorably expressed it: 'If the euro fails, then Europe fails.' But is the euro really the foundation on which Europe stands? It is possible that shares and exports could collapse without taking the common currency down with them, but are persuasive economic benefits the reason why we believe in Europe? Wasn't there something more? Something like freedom, emancipation and the participation of all people in the commonweal – no matter what their gender, ethnicity, religion or sexual orientation?

As a writer, I regularly visit schools, and there I almost always talk about Europe. I don't tell the students that Europe will give them an apprenticeship or a cool job. I don't point out how convenient it is to travel without a passport or having to exchange money. The students come up with the material advantages of Europe all by themselves, without demanding too much of Europe, without expecting the apprenticeship or the cool job. Nor do I talk to them about peace. Everyone knows that Europe has brought the continent peace – but no one would believe me if I threatened, as the British premier did once more in a moment of panic, that without Europe war would rage once more. I do not tell them how, when I was at school, my classmates had trouble finding French host families for an exchange with our partner school in Lorraine because the French grandparents didn't want a German in the house, whereas I, as an immigrants' child, was welcome everywhere. To young

Germans today, it seems highly theoretical that they might have been personae non gratae in France.

No: I tell them, Look around you. Look at all the different places your parents come from, how different you all look, what different names you have. Look in your neighbourhood, look at the national football squad, look at the refugees (and if anyone is sympathetic towards the refugees today, it is schoolchildren; that gives me strength every time): think about how it would be if Germany went back to defining itself as an ethnic nation. Or France. Or England. Would that be a portrayal of your reality, the society you grew up in? Think about what a Europe of Fatherlands would mean, the lands of their fathers that the right-wing populists always talk about: how many of you would no longer belong to this country? And what about those schools in which Germany is only very few children's 'fatherland'? Do you really think they could all be kicked out, or demoted to second-class citizens? Or would they leave of their own accord – and where would they go?

And then I can see, every time, the students' brains whirring as they look around, as they think, and also ask questions or raise objections, ask for details. Immediately a discussion begins, especially since the cultural diversity of today's Western European societies is only the beginning. When I ask the students whether, in all seriousness, they want to reinstate discrimination against homosexuality, and someone making rules about who and when and how they're allowed to love? Whether they want to read only German literature in school, explained only by Germans? Whether they think climate change is a hoax, whether they've thought about introducing the death penalty, or abolishing the separation of powers? What has that got to do with Europe? the students then ask me. That has a great deal to do with Europe, I reply; just look at the platforms of the anti-European parties:

they're not just about Islam and foreigners; they're against exactly the society you're growing up in, against your teachers who are liberal, against your mayors who are providing aid to refugees, against fighting climate change, against minorities' rights, equal opportunity, and your history curriculum which does not make excuses for German guilt; against you who are today's Germany, a European Germany at last.

Of course, the right-wing populists use the word freedom, talk about self-determination, demand referendums. But by that they do not mean what the Enlightenment meant: that freedom always means freedom for those with different opinions, different beliefs, different looks, different loves, and not the despotism of the majority. They do not hold the human dignity of every person to be inviolable, but only some people's. Apparently not the dignity of your classmate if – like the vice-chairman of the AfD party, Alexander Gauland – they do not want him living in their neighbourhood because of his skin colour, even if he plays on the national team.

I can't claim that I leave the students all singing the 'Ode to Joy' when I go. The opposite is rather the case: I learn from them that you do not have to have lived through the war to have a biographical experience of the necessity of Europe. The 75 per cent of young Britons who voted against Brexit – it would have been 80 or 90 per cent in Germany – are an injunction to all of us who will pass on the European project to our children, unless we do not. We should stop listening to those who are already spouting polemics against lofty speeches because they themselves can only think as small as David Cameron. Mark Rutte, the current president of the European Council, who was elected only in the Netherlands, says he doesn't want 'the Europe of the lofty speeches' nor 'any more big visions, conventions and treaties'. That is exactly what we have heard since the failed constitution – and after every other crisis: still less Europe, and for God's sake no visions. It is this pragmatism, with an eye only on one's own national electorate, that has hamstrung Europe. Those who want to weaken Europe further out of fear of Europe's opponents are playing into those opponents' hands.

'We owe the prosperity, the security and the peace that we enjoy here today to those who, seventy years ago, put their shared interests above their particular interests, appealing to what they have in common instead of their differences' – those are not the words of a politically resurrected Giscard d'Estaing but a post that suddenly appeared on the Facebook page of my seventeen-year-old daughter, who is really not as political as all that. I could hardly believe my eyes last weekend when she showed me the text, which has been shared more times than any other post of hers. And the comments under her post, and the countless other pages of young people from every part of Europe which my daughter showed me next were equally inspired with the European idea, in words no one of the older generation dares to use. 'This here is our future', my daughter wrote, 'because we the young Europeans, are the ones who will have to live tomorrow with the consequences of today's decisions, and who therefore have to fight to preserve what we have grown up with.' Yes, I said, so fight, and not just online – and also don't forget where your commas go. I would rather listen to the three-quarters of young Britons than the president of the council, who was not above making deals with right-wing populists to take over the government in 2010.

Yes, Mr Rutte, what Europe needs now is a refounding, a thoroughly thought-out, carefully crafted structure instead of a permanent interim expedient. It needs a constitution which will give democratic legitimacy and transparency to its decisions; it needs a parliament worthy of the name that will create a European public sphere; in the long run it needs

Europe-wide parties, or at least party alliances, that actually stand together in European elections. Instead of twenty-eight commissioners it needs active bodies, and instead of veto powers it needs clear rules on treaty violations. It needs an economy with not just a common market but a common policy which permits intervention in national budgets, but which also provides for fair fiscal equalization and the convergence of standards of living. That will be expensive for Germany in particular, but not nearly as expensive as the debt policy. Europe needs a clear definition and strict boundaries on what its remit is and what is better decided in the member countries, the regions and the cities. It doesn't have to take care of everything, but it must be able to take care of the little that is its part. It needs a foundation that will support it in the next generation. And then let the people vote! Not every British voter who voted for Brexit is a nationalist, and many of those who preferred in the end to remain in the EU choked back their anger to do so because this Europe that David Cameron represented had opportunism written all over its face.

A democratic, fair, efficient and explicitly not omnipotent union, on the other hand, would surely win majorities – not immediately and everywhere, but in the founding member countries and in enough other countries – even in Poland, where for months hundreds of thousands of people have been marching in the streets with EU flags for the preservation of their democracy. And the other countries would follow and return as soon as they recognize how much they have to gain from political community. It was the bond with the European project that first allowed democracy to succeed in Germany; it was the pressure from Europe that contributed crucially to overturning the dictatorships in the south of the continent: in Spain, Portugal, Greece; it was the prospect of belonging to Europe that later motivated the

Eastern European states, and most recently the Balkan countries, to introduce democratic reforms. Europe can continue in future to be a promise.

Yes, it takes time to give the European Union a new, more stable foundation; it takes composure. At the same time, the people in Strasbourg, Luxembourg and Brussels now know very well what a functioning Europe would have to look like: after all, they have suffered long enough under the design flaws of the Treaty of Lisbon. And if we can propose a new charter for Europe fast enough, perhaps even the United Kingdom could participate in the decision, as long as the United Kingdom still exists.

24

What We Can Do in This Situation

After the Attacks in Ansbach, Würzburg and Munich

Frankfurter Allgemeine Zeitung, 2 August 2016

It is not just the dramatic news that is worrying these days when you turn on the special reports on television in the evening or click from page to page on the internet because the next day's newspapers will be out of date when they arrive: the unprecedented series of attacks which started in Nice and has now reached Germany, raising the question, even in refugee aid initiatives, how many terrorists there are among the refugees; the coup and counter-coup in Turkey; at the same time, the nomination of Donald Trump as the Republican Party's candidate for president of the United States; a short time before, Brexit. It is the vague feeling that these events and developments are related without anyone being able to say exactly how.

There won't be an immediate causal relation, except perhaps on the internet, where of course the end of the world, or sometimes the end of Western civilization, is predicted every year. At the same time, the intervals in the breaking news are too short to allow a clean separation of the events in our minds. If we then read the next morning what the newspapers report on the inside pages, we really get frightened: the siege of Aleppo and the virtual termination of peace negotiations in Geneva by the reinvigorated Syrian government; Putin's accusations of conspiracy over the doping investigations, and, on the other side, Obama's accusations of conspiracy over the e-mail revelations just in time for the Democrats' convention; the upcoming referendum against refugees in Hungary; the FPÖ's successful challenge of the presidential election in Austria and the predicted victory of its candidate Norbert Hofer when the election is repeated; before that, state legislative elections in Germany again in which the AfD can be expected to show that they are capable of spectacular electoral results in spite of their internal self-demolition. What if they had a charismatic leader? On the horizon is Marine Le Pen as a potential president of France in 2017.

You have only to lean back a moment and recall how much we thought unimaginable a year ago, or at most remotely possible in a very abstract future, and you begin to see it all as a bad dream – from a million refugees within just a few months to New Years' Eve in Cologne to the random murders in German inner cities; from the annulment of an election in Austria to the suddenly possible end of the EU to an American president who abrogates the mutual defence agreement of NATO while at the same time fraternizing with Putin, Erdoğan and the right-wing populists of Europe. But no, it is not a dream, it is reality, and if anything was dreamlike it was the long period of unadulterated harmony that had dominated Western Europe since the end of the Cold War, while in other regions of the globe the social, political and religious conflicts escalated.

The United States have already learned, on 11 September 2001, that not even a space-based missile defence system could guard against all the dangers in the world. And not only there, but still more in Israel we can study how terror, if it lasts, can change societies and radicalize their politics. Its striking power, the number of its supporters and their ideological steadfastness are not the decisive factors. The crucial thing is that the terror can strike anyone. Because, in contrast to the classic forms of political violence, the most recent attacks have been aimed at civilians, responsible organizations are no longer needed, and even the motives keep changing in the news crawl: psychopaths; Islamists; now in Munich apparently a right-wing radical who hated foreigners, refugees, Muslims, although he himself is vaguely perceived as a foreigner, a refugee, a Muslim.

And this insecurity – or simply the fear of going to a concert, the train station or a political assembly; the fear for one's children – sets events in a relation that becomes causality: jihadism encourages right-wing populism, which in turn weakens the European Union; Brexit makes Putin happy, and he expresses his growing self-assurance through military aid to the Syrian regime, whose air strikes continue to drive people to flee; Erdoğan's autocratic rule increases Turkey's distance from Europe, which reduces the opportunities for keeping refugees away from Europe; the problems of integrating the refugees become arguments for the opponents of Europe. Even Ukraine is still a part of this complex because it threatens to become a negligible quantity: after all, refugees and terrorists make it more urgent to find a solution for Syria, which is only possible in consultation with Russia. And no one can be bothered at the moment about poor Yemen, which is sinking in chaos and death, because Saudi Arabia is already angry enough over the West's understanding with Iran; that in turn is necessary in order to rein in Tehran's nuclear ambitions; the nuclear deal becomes a burden for Hillary Clinton's campaign with every new missile test by the Iranian Revolutionary Guards, while Trump ... and so on. Oh, and there was something or other in Afghanistan, too.

The historian Tobias Stone reminds us these days in his much discussed blog that the various events and developments which led to the great political disasters of the modern period have been seen only in hindsight as related; those who lived through them were surprised at each successive escalation, the consequences of which were out of all proportion to their causes – as the seventeen million dead of the First World War were to the assassination of Franz Ferdinand in Sarajevo. Stone then considers what might constitute such a Franz Ferdinand moment in the near future – and arrives at thought experiments that are disturbingly plausible if we assume, for example, a victory for Donald Trump in the American presidential election or further spectacular terrorist attacks in Europe. Not every smouldering fire flares up into an inferno, and there are probably far more historical examples of dangerous situations which resolved themselves instead of leading to humanitarian disasters – but they are not so well remembered. After all, panic that proves unfounded is always somewhat embarrassing.

Looking only at my own lifetime, the world seemed to be near its end in the early 1980s with the threat of nuclear war. Then, as now, different developments coincided which were only vaguely related but nonetheless caused a general feeling of anxiety: the Islamic Revolution in Iran and, with it, the humiliation of America; the Russian invasion of Afghanistan; the meltdown at Three Mile Island; acid rain and dying forests; the nuclear arms race; Reagan, Thatcher and – yes, the fears evoked in my pacifist circles by the conservative turn more than thirty years ago are hardly believable today – Helmut Kohl. The film *The Day After*, about the consequences of a nuclear strike, seemed to us a kind of magic lantern affording a glimpse of the immediate future, comparable in its influence with Houellebecq's novel *Submission* – and today the film is rightly forgotten, because it was not well made and because what happened in reality was not the end of the world but the fall of the Iron Curtain. But, at the same time, the concern over nuclear war, environmental destruction, Islamism and so on played a part in bringing the 1980s to a more than moderate ending – indeed, a hopeful one. The fact that hopes can be dashed is perhaps the most constant condition of human experience and not a reason not to have new hopes in the first place.

History doesn't happen; history is made. To take only the most obvious example, which is connected, however vaguely, with everything else – because less fear of terrorist attacks would make the right-wing populists . . . et cetera – it is possible to defeat the 'Islamic State' and to draw a blueprint for peace in Syria. It is possible for Islamic institutions not just to condemn terror but to critically confront Wahhabism, which is the philosophical foundation of the IS. It is equally possible for Western countries not to choose as their closest Middle Eastern ally Saudi Arabia, which spreads Wahhabism as far as the mosques of Molenbeek and Bonn. In Germany, it is possible to speed up asylum applications so that young men are not kept waiting for months and years, in provisional shelters, with no employment, for their future to begin. It is possible to restrict the purchase of firearms and to outlaw the most murderous internet games; it is possible for society to repudiate them. It is possible to reform the European Union so that it finds more approval again, with two-speed rules if necessary. It is possible to develop a common European refugee policy that protects the borders and distributes the burdens and grants asylum to those who are truly in need instead of selecting the physically strongest, giving preference to young single men because they are the most likely to survive the dangers and hardships of the irregular migration routes. It is possible to fight climate change, which otherwise will produce much greater migrations of refugees, as when whole countries sink below sea level, or the deserts in sub-Saharan Africa continue to expand so rapidly.

All these things are possible, and of course it is illusory to hope that all of them will be realized, and at the same time. But preventing the worst does not mean everything must turn out for the best; putting out a few fires could be enough to prevent the smouldering from becoming a conflagration. If the 'Islamic State' with its barely 30,000 fighters were defeated, for example, and its leaders tried and convicted, there would still be young men in Europe who are susceptible to jihadism – but there would no longer be a triumphant narrative in which they could enrol. Losers rapidly decline in appeal, as al-Qaeda found to its dismay, and propaganda videos, middlemen, sponsors and training camps in Europe's immediate vicinity are important even for individual perpetrators, as the investigations after the Ansbach suicide bombing revealed. The lone-wolf terrorists are not so lone after all.

This is not an appeal for military intervention, nor for German air strikes, but an appeal to finally realize the global urgency of a peaceful solution for Syria and Iraq. In those two countries, the state must begin representing the population again to some extent in order to confront the terrorists effectively. But that also entails a dialogue between the various actors' foreign protectors. That is why, immediately after the incursion of IS in Iraq, Germany's foreign minister Steinmeier proposed a kind of CSCE for the Middle East. Two years later, a solution to the various Middle East conflicts is hardly conceivable in smaller dimensions than that. It sounds unrealistic? Perhaps. But later no one will understand why there was not at least an attempt at peace today. It is also clear, however, that the opponents of the 'Islamic State' need military support as long as the war goes on – and note that this does not mean Bashar al-Assad's army, which has recently fought some battles against IS but much more resolutely attacks the other rebel groups or, to be more exact, the Sunni population.

A consequence of the present situation, which in Germany is perceived to be as dramatic as any moment since the war, is the spreading realization that we are not isolated from the rest of the world. After all, the conflagration has long since begun in large parts of the Middle East and Africa: failed states, ethnic cleansing, mass murder, assassinations, the pollution of whole regions, the growing gap between rich and poor, and with it the decline of the middle class, the lack of prospects of well-educated youth, and much more. Terror and the social upheaval of globalization have long since reached France, Belgium and Britain too, and in Israel and Palestine the younger generation no longer know what it feels like to live in safety. Why should Germany happen to remain economically and socially unaffected by the times we live in? And yet Germany, thanks to its intact rule of law and its relative social equilibrium, has better chances than many other countries of preserving its freedoms. What is more, with its increased prestige in the world and its economic power, Germany has opportunities to influence the course of history, however minimally. The German foreign minister could reiterate his proposal: presented at the highest level, supported by Europe, it might be heard this time.

There will continue to be attacks in future even without the 'Islamic State'. The idea that nihilistic terror is inherent in modern society can be found as early as Dostoevsky, and the end of the industrial age, together with the fragmentation of the public sphere, is once more producing new pathologies which could become murderous. But what makes the IS so incendiary is that it enables an individual to exert an influence on global politics. This is the difference between jihadism and the phantasms that right-wing murderers invent to give their destructive urges a larger meaning; it is what makes jihadism so much more appealing to losers and unstable personalities, and not just in Europe. What state, what culture, what religion could we declare war upon if a hate criminal were to rise up as a saviour of the West? And yet the meaning that an Islamist attacker invokes is very real: it refers to a state, a highly effective propaganda machine and an ideology, Wahhabism, which is preached in mosques all over the world, with or without the incitement to violence. When an attacker claims to represent 1.4 billion Muslims, there are more and more people, and by now political parties and the potential next president of the United States, who are ready to believe him. Those who shout 'Allahu akbar' as they kill can write history.

The *New York Times* published a dossier last week that puts faces to all the 247 people who died about the same time in mid-March in jihadist attacks in Belgium, Turkey, Pakistan, the Ivory Coast and Nigeria; at an airport, in a subway station, in streets and squares, in a bus, in a park, in a sold-out football stadium, in a holiday resort and in a mosque. These victims did not belong to any single culture, faith or nation – when you look at their faces, look at their clothes, read their biographies, learn their dreams and what they were busy with when they were robbed of their lives, they form almost a kind of family album of humanity in our time. And when the terror of the 'Islamic State' struck Ansbach in Bavaria, it was a few hours after an IS suicide bomber in Kabul had blown up eighty peaceful demonstrators and wounded 250. Only when we understand that we are all being attacked together, whether we live in Bavaria or in Afghanistan, will we be able to defend ourselves together.

25

THE WEIGHT OF TWO SACKS

In Search of the Last Blind Spots of Progress in China

Die Zeit, 16 January 2020

The realization comes with a pole which has a white plastic sack tied to each end. We have met many peasants on our trek, mostly women, carrying such a pole across their shoulders, their backs bowed, their arms extended like a cross. Before that, we saw them out of the windows of the bullet trains and walking along the emergency stopping lanes of the brand-new motorways that eat their way like worms through the nearly impassable mountain ranges. Even on the bridges that span the valleys many hundreds of metres above the ground for convenient transit, we sped past the walking crucifixes, and in the countless tunnels their sacks shone in our headlights for a quarter or a half second, unreal like a dream vision. Stopping lane – the word takes on a whole new meaning when the motorway tunnel becomes a roofed track between the farmers' fields. Because our headlights also light up peasants, mostly women, pausing for a moment beside the sacks they have set down. Out of exhaustion? That was not discernible in the quarter or half second we saw them.

The transport routes that China is rapidly building up and down the country represent progress not only for the city-dwellers: the railway network of the bullet trains, 350 km per hour, now measures some 25,500 kilometres of track, and on Google Maps the motorways already look like a fine-meshed sieve. It is not only the pedlars and the itinerant labourers who are glad, and comfortable too, as their coaches roll rapidly along; so are the many millions of Chinese schoolchildren who live at boarding schools during the week and the students on visits home. Even the poorest people benefit, although in ways not promised by state television and the investment market reports. They no longer have to climb over the mountains with their poles weighed down by sacks to get to the markets: now they can go right through them. And a Chinese peasant's life is hard enough anyway, so they are not about to worry about lung cancer from the exhaust fumes.

The landscape we are travelling through, on foot and by public transport, could not be more picturesque; the wooded slopes so steep and the mountaintops so round, as if God had painted sugarloaves green; streams, waterfalls and enchanted-looking fields of sweet potatoes, maize or tea hidden here and there in the forests. Where the hills become flatter and the valleys broader, the mountainsides are terraced with rice paddies, the most beautiful cultivation of land anywhere. The water from which the plants sprout up glitters in the play of sunlight and clouds like an ethereal mosaic. Especially for my twelve-year-old daughter, it is fun to search along the narrow ridges between the paddies for the one trail that leads downwards a level, and ultimately to the valley floor. And then the villages, sprinkled among the woods or between the wet fields that look like pools you could dive into: all the houses still made of wood, with gables like those on postcards and verandas where a person could enjoy the view. And the silence, when everywhere else China confronts you with an incessant bustle: often even the main lanes are too narrow for cars, but hardly anyone drives cars here anyway; mopeds and scooters more likely, and those only in the past few years. We were in one village that didn't even have paved lanes, and it took two hours to get there up the mountain trails. From up there, China's aggressive advance into the future feels more than just a day's journey away – rather a century, in fact.

We had been curious about the last blind spots of the progress that has left hardly a stone standing in China: those who recall the photographs from the 1980s – masses of cyclists passing flat brick houses – will no longer recognize metropolises such as Beijing and Shanghai, which seem to consist of nothing but motorways and tower blocks, shopping malls, neon lights and gigantic public transport stops. Even minor district capitals that were little more than big villages a few decades ago now have a million inhabitants and taller buildings than Berlin or Paris. And the building continues incessantly; in the provinces especially, the country looks like one big building site; the train repeatedly races past whole forests of giant cranes. We had been curious about the other side of the coin, a China that has not yet experienced the boom, with its own rituals and its old arts, a side that is no doubt poor but may also be worth preserving – and someone had mentioned Qiandongnan, where many small minorities live, each with its own language, its own songs and its own religion. There, if anywhere, we would find a world that hadn't been ploughed under even by communism. Most of the other people we asked, writers, professors and journalists, had never even heard of the mountainous region in southwestern China: that struck us as a good omen. And, in fact, in some villages we aren't even identified as foreigners, because another world than China is beyond all imagination. Different as we are in looks and language, the people assume we are another minority from some far-off part of the huge country.

The realization comes with a pole which has a white plastic sack tied to each end. Everywhere along the way, between the fields where we stop to rest, in the villages where we spend the night, the peasants, and mostly the women, complain of the physical exertion, the deprivation, the lack of money. Working in construction, on the assembly line or as a cleaner is so much better, they say; that's why the young people all go away; the men especially travel from city to city. The privation of the three hundred million Chinese on whose mobility, low aspirations and low wages the economic growth is substantially built fills special reports in the Western press. But whenever we asked migrant workers on their visits home in recent days, we heard rejoicing at having escaped rural life.

Why is that? we asked the thirty-year-old Xie Liying, who is familiar with both worlds because she and her husband travelled from factory to factory until their son reached school age and they returned to their house in Dongmeng, one of the best-preserved villages anywhere in the region, which is now promoting eco-tourism. The inhabitants have agreed to the suggestion from the little, tasteful hotel, which bought a small plot of land from the community and also contributes a few good jobs, to wear their colourful traditional dress as often as possible to further beautify Dongmeng. The Yao cultivate their rituals and songs anyway, as all the minorities do.

And yet Xie Liying is unhappy to be back. Dongmeng is where she comes from; she has known her neighbours here all her life; everyone here speaks her language and in the evening they all sing together, always the same songs, always with new verses they improvise on the spot; here she wears the elaborate clothes that she sews herself; here she owns a house and her own fields, eats the food she grows herself, enjoys the full aroma with no artificial flavours; only here does she have clean air to breathe and beauty all around her:

the beauty of nature, of the architecture, the traditions and the artisanship. Xie Liying leads a life that could hardly be more authentic; she sets her own daily routine; she has all she wants to eat, by her own account; only here does she have health insurance and a free school for her son – so why is she nostalgic for the niche where the three of them lived, and where they could have been evicted at any moment, for the extreme insecurity and dependency, for the monotony of the factory, the same hand movement ten hours a day, six days a week, for the strange world of concrete and tar, her only entertainment videos on her smartphone instead of the community singing that enchants even foreign travellers?

I don't like physical labour, she says.

But the work on the assembly line is physical too, I interject.

But there, there was food and money. Here there is only food. I would like to buy clothes sometimes, eat something different sometimes, instead of always just rice, potatoes and maize. Besides, the assembly line is something different from carrying heavy sacks and standing in mud every day.

And your son?

That's why we came back, the only reason: so he can go to school and later move to the city. This is not a good life here.

Was it better before?

My parents still lived in huts with walls made of reeds; it was always wet inside in the rainy season. And my grandparents still starved, really starved, every day. There used to be robbers; people hardly dared go out to the fields. And the women had to bear their child alone, all alone, and no one but the mother was allowed to touch the baby for thirty days; that was the tradition. Many mothers died; it was terrible, for the children too. No, sir, it is getting better, ever better; my son will have it better than we do.

We listened to Xie Liying; we listened to many peasants in Qiandongnan, mostly women. It was not easy for them to talk to strangers about their feelings, about hopes or fears, but as soon as we asked practical questions they started telling their stories. How long does it take you to sew a dress: a year; what is that song about: love, of course; who taught you to play that horn: our horn master; do people drink this much rice wine every day: no, only on the feast days – alcohol is not a problem here; how much does the tea sell for: the equivalent of 600 euros per harvest, thanks to chemical fertilizer and the new premium varieties that the city-dwellers crave; or, for that matter, would you rather work on a building site or in the fields? And every time, all the young people and most of the old people, all the men and most of the women answer: the future is better than the past; progress is a blessing; the bleak life of a wage-earner that we think is so alienated is always preferred to their original lifestyle in their magnificent homeland. I am not the only one who is discreetly disappointed every time; being critical of contemporary culture, as the author I am, I don't want to believe it; nor do our two travelling companions from Shanghai and Beijing, much less my daughter, who at home in Germany strictly insists on organic labels when we shop and demonstrates for climate action every Friday.

Finally we speak to a woman, fifty, sixty years old if her furrowed face does not deceive us, panting as she ploughs a potato field. But she doesn't understand us, nor we her, because she speaks only the language of the Miao, one of the many ethnic groups in Qiandongnan. So she shrugs her shoulders before taking up her hoe again and turning away.

We continue along the uneven path that follows the river, below the rice terraces and far away from the villages, which are a few hundred metres higher. Beside the path are two upright sacks, connected by a long pole; they probably belong to the old peasant woman who is still ploughing her field a hundred metres behind us. Absent-mindedly, I go to lift the pole as I pass, and I snap back because the sacks don't move a centimetre. Only when I grip the pole with both hands, as if I were a weight-lifter, am I able to raise the sacks up in the air. Unthinkable that I would lay the pole across my shoulders and then march mile after mile, over rough terrain up the mountain to the village or through a motorway tunnel to the nearest market. I set the sacks down and lift up my daughter to estimate the weight: my daughter weighs 34 kilos; the sacks are much heavier, unbelievably much heavier for an old woman. I don't like the physical labour, Xie Liying told us, many others told us, and finally I understand, as I look at the rice terraces on the opposite mountainside, at the river flowing through the valley, the villages in such splendid harmony with the natural surroundings, the sky that is still clean: no one here is happy to live from the work of their own hands.

We haven't seen a car all day, nor even a moped; not one asphalted road. Only peasants in their fields, who waded through the water that is fortunately only knee-deep to chop a path for us along the level riverbank when there was no way to go forwards across the slope. Suddenly a column of huge excavating machines comes towards us along the riverbed, their drivers looking as astonished as we are. They may still be wondering today who the strange-looking figures with the rucksack and the child were, but we found our answer just past the next bend in the river: a dam is being built, lining the idyllic valley with bare concrete on three sides to a height of a hundred, two hundred metres. There are hardly any remote areas left in China. Except for the high mountains and the deserts, even the most desolate spots are hardly ever less than 50 kilometres from the motorway, the bullet trains, the airports, the former provincial towns that are megalopolises today. And where there is still nature, it is exploited and industrialized, if not for tourism, then to meet the constantly growing energy demand. While economic growth is seen in the cities at least as two-edged, what with air pollution, noise and rising rents, it is still eagerly longed for in the countryside.

None of the construction workers we talk to would trade their wages, the equivalent of 13 euros a day, to go back to the fields. And in the village that is still completely conserved in the traditional wooden building style, but now lies adjacent to the concrete desert of the future reservoir, the inhabitants are glad of the dam because it is bringing them temporary jobs, better transport connections, and buyers for local products in the form of workers, engineers and suppliers. Fewer necks will be bowed under the sack-laden poles on the way to the nearest market.

And freedom? Those who have no access to foreign media learn nothing about the concentration camps for the Uyghurs, the rebellion in Hong Kong or the growing censorship. Those whose parents have at most a primary-school education dream not of elections but of A-levels. Those who still remember going hungry as children – to them freedom means, first of all, enough to eat. Unlike the newly industrialized democracies such as India and Indonesia, where economic growth is similar but hardly benefits the rural population and hence the majority, crumbs of China's prosperity fall even in the remote provinces. Because fighting poverty is not just a side effect that may or may not occur but is, rather, like the bullet trains, motorways and dams, an explicit agenda, or indeed the primary goal of a party that derives its legitimacy not from elections but from statistics: from growth, prosperity, efficiency. There must be no country in the world that has fought abject misery as successfully as China has within one generation: where forty years ago nine out of ten citizens still lived in extreme poverty – some nine hundred million people – by the World Bank's calculations, not even 2 per cent do now. The results of Western developmental aid, or the structural reforms imposed by the International Monetary Fund in its member countries, are not apt to teach Beijing any lessons. And the water tanks and fire hoses that stand ready in every village may be a minor detail. But in southern Asia and South America, I have seen hardly a trace of fire safety provision, which makes progress as tangible to the inhabitants as the light from the solar-powered streetlamps.

Even behind the tourism that is growing as rapidly as the cities, there is a plan in Qiandongnan such as one often misses among the holiday high-rises on the Mediterranean Sea. The bed-and-breakfasts in traditional architecture where we spent most of our nights are subsidized by the state to give the inhabitants an incentive to stay in their villages. And where it is too expensive to build streets and schools, the villages are offered the option of moving en bloc. Most of them accept it. The new settlements, which can be seen every few kilometres along the equally new highways, may not be exactly picturesque. However, they have drains, bus stops and broadband internet.

Of course, the villagers' world that we are hiking through will disappear or be preserved in part by tourism. The slopes in Qiandongnan are too steep and the fields too small for the industrialized agriculture that the big businesses are interested in. The old people will die here in their wooden houses, but almost all of the young are seeking their fortunes elsewhere. They come home only to visit for the festivals. But when none of their relatives are left in the villages, the songs will be forgotten or will survive only as folklore. What communism could not do – plough up Qiandongnan – will be accomplished by capitalism. The richness in ethnicities, languages, rituals and traditions will be lost. But only the grandchildren will complain about that, or more likely the great-grandchildren, who will have no memory of the heavy weight of the two sacks.

From Baiyan Cun, where we stop for the night, the long, mournful tones of horns reporting the death of a villager waft out to meet us. The women hornblowers provide the monotonous bass line, the men the droning melody which pulls at us more strongly the closer we come to the dead man's house. There is no religion in Qiandongnan in our sense of the word, as a system of beliefs. Religion consists mainly of practices that situate one's own time in the continuum of eternity. In front of some houses there are elaborately carved coffins that call attention now to a person's inevitable future death. Those who are ill seek help not only from medicine but also from spirits. And the dead are honoured with feasts that never seem to end. Seven days and nights the horns blow, and the relatives and neighbours dance in a circle around the cooled Plexiglas coffin in which the deceased is laid out. For the Miao, funerals are the most important celebrations in their lives. The whole village helps to prepare plenty to eat for the mourners, including those from the surrounding villages. Ten women are assigned just to cutting the vegetables, ten more to the cooking, while the men divide up the shopping and the butchering of the animals. Getting enough to eat is by no means taken for granted in Qiandongnan; the abundance that there is at least on feast days is celebrated all the more extravagantly.

In the past, we hear, they danced and played music with empty stomachs. Were those more admirable celebrations? No! comes the startled answer. The children, it seems certain, will no longer be honoured for seven days and nights after their death.

26

For Three Dollars a Day
After the West's Withdrawal from Afghanistan
Frankfurter Allgemeine Zeitung, 26 August 2021

Among the many lies that accompanied the Western mission in Afghanistan, the biggest is probably this one: It was about liberating the Afghans. No, it was about interests, and that's what it had been about from the start. Just as Iran and Pakistan are doing, as Russia, India and, by now, China too are doing, the Western community of nations was pursuing with all its might its own strategic, political and economic interests in the Hindu Kush, as everywhere else in the world. Nor is there anything wrong with that, as long as the resulting policy does not grossly violate their self-imposed obligations, values and laws.

The United States did not liberate Germany out of concern for the Jews. It did not intervene militarily until the moment it had become unmistakable that Hitler's Germany was a menace to the whole world, and hence to America itself. And, after its victory, the United States did not reconstruct West Germany out of love for the Germans. In opposition to public opinion at the time and to forces, including some within its own democratic camp, that preferred deindustrializing, disarming or even depopulating Germany, the government in Washington invested in making the ruined and demoralized country into a friend and a strategic partner in the middle of Europe. That was far-sighted; it was extremely successful – but it was not altruistic. Except for short-term aid in cases of natural disasters or famines, which even dictatorships regularly grant, states never act selflessly.

Afghanistan had stood in the focus of global politics once before: during the 'Great Game' of the late nineteenth century, when the British Empire and tsarist Russia strove for dominance in the Hindu Kush. But afterwards, from the 1920s, when it seemed a remote, somehow languorous country to the rest of the world, Afghanistan developed not too badly. General elections were introduced; a secularly oriented bourgeoisie formed in the cities; the bureaucracy functioned tolerably. There was a government and not just a Potemkin village. The trucks that Mercedes-Benz built in Afghanistan were exported to India; the proportion of women at the universities increased from year to year; and the jazz clubs were considered the best in the Middle East. True, the people in the countryside were desperately poor; archaic customs prevailed in the villages; but at least the country was largely self-sufficient, literacy was spreading – progress was visible. Many Western travellers since the 1960s have discovered Afghanistan as the land of their dreams, where they were welcome everywhere and – something inconceivable today – able to travel safely even in the remotest provinces. Peace reigned!

That changed dramatically when the Soviet Union, in the course of the East–West conflict, wanted to expand its sphere of influence and make Afghanistan its vassal – first with the 1978 coup against Mohammed Daoud Khan and then with the 1979 invasion of the Red Army when the new communist government had come under pressure. The United States under its new president Ronald Reagan reacted promptly, of course, by financing the Mujahidin, along with

Pakistan and the Wahhabi Gulf states. In other words, the military engagement of the West began not in 2001 with the invasion but more than forty years ago. And, from the beginning, it was closely tied to the radical political Islam that was systematically supported as an opposing force to the Soviet Union. The middle class, the foundation of any democracy, were ground down by both sides, driven out of the country, demeaned and killed.

Only after the victory of the Mujahidin did the West's Afghanistan policy reach its low point, however. That victory did not bring the peace that the West had hoped for, the peace which would allow it to pursue business interests in Afghanistan, to access the immense mineral resources, control the entire region's water supply and establish a stable ally at the crossroads of Iran, Russia and China. Washington unscrupulously supported its allies Pakistan and Saudi Arabia in building up the much more radical, Sunni extremist Taliban, who took the country almost without resistance thanks to American assault rifles, a bulging war chest and a terrified, war-weary population. The terror that ensued cannot be called medieval without doing injustice to the Middle Ages. But the world did not take notice of it until the terror spilled over on 11 September 2001. Western realpolitik had caused the greatest possible realpolitical damage. So George W. Bush read Khaled Hosseini's *Kite Runner* and Tony Blair moved the British pop celebrities to tears with his sermon on women's rights and democracy. But the crazy thing is – it could have worked.

Because the West once possessed this strategic advantage over all the other competing powers: most people in the world, Muslims included, would rather live in the Western-dominated hemisphere than in Russia, in China or, for that matter, under Islamist rule. This is strikingly visible in the refugee routes, and thus in these days at Kabul's airport: the

Afghans are not trying to get to such countries as China, Russia, Pakistan, Iran or Saudi Arabia, which would be much nearer; they are camping at the airport in the hope of somehow getting to that West which is allegedly so bitterly hated. And thus the prospect of living in a halfway democratic, independent but politically Western-oriented state, in which human rights are respected, women attain more and more participation in public life, and a plural, critical public sphere exists, released tremendous energy among the Afghans after the liberation from the Taliban. The voter turnout, even in spite of great dangers, was spectacularly high; the media landscape was the freest and the most vital in the entire region and, in contrast to the first Taliban reign, parents are insisting on their daughters' right to education today even in the remotest villages.

Yes, the corruption in Afghanistan was and is breathtaking; no wonder, after the West handed over the country to its most corrupt men – warlords and drug barons – in order to avoid fighting with their own ground troops. True, the pace of development was more than just sluggish: twenty years after the beginning of the Western engagement, many roads are in worse condition than under the Taliban, and there are tremendous gaps in health-care provision as well as in electrical power and water supply. Except in the education sector, the result of the Western deployment is disastrous. The construction boom of recent years in the cities, the new shopping malls, restaurants and gated communities – these are not signs of a healthy economy but financed in large part by opium, which has been cultivated unchecked again since the beginning of the Western withdrawal in 2014.

The West's engagement, however, for all the euphonious affirmations and stylish PowerPoint presentations, has always followed a military logic, and accordingly the proportion of military spending to civil aid was seven to one. And of the comparatively few billions that actually arrived in Afghanistan, the vast majority flowed back in the form of contracts to multinational businesses, commissions to sub- and sub-subcontractors, materials that were almost entirely imported, wages for foreign workers, down to catering, for which every onion was flown in from abroad. There was much talk of NATO, but never of the Nepalese mercenaries who guarded the Western soldiers and the highly paid security services, and who were also charged against the available budget. The imported water that a Western advisor drank cost more than an Afghan doctor earned: three dollars a day on average. James Dobbins, the special envoy for Afghanistan under President George W. Bush, summed up the American involvement in the country thus: 'The main lesson of Afghanistan is: low input, low output'; Afghanistan was 'in manpower and money the least resourced American nation-building effort in our history.'

Afghanistan is not an example of the failure of developmental aid. Rather, the past twenty years show in detail – as documented in numerous reports, including official government evaluations – the kind of fiasco that results when aid is commercialized from the ground up and ultimately serves domestic profits. And now the failure of a perverted reconstruction industry and the disaster that Trump's and also, sadly, Biden's nationalism have wrought are presented as an argument for putting one's own house in order and no more. Instead of such crude analyses, which as a rule are devoid of all knowledge of local conditions, it would be more important to ask why, since the end of the East–West conflict, one Western mission after another has gone haywire. Because keeping reality at bay is not an option anyway. Reality comes crashing down on us, as it did in the autumn of 2015, when we thought peace would return to Syria all by itself and the good Lord would provide for the several million refugees at Europe's gates.

Now, too, what we are seeing is not the consequences of our involvement but the opposite, the consequences of our withdrawal: the fact that the violence is escalating and the Taliban have been able to grow in strength was the immediate consequence of a foreign policy that Donald Trump sold as 'America First', while in fact he was pursuing the shrinking and hence the disempowerment of America – it was not for nothing that the Russian intelligence agency had supported his election campaign. When Washington began to negotiate with the Taliban directly without even consulting the elected Afghan government, it was clear to the Afghans who would end up in power. In a country dominated for over forty years by war, and hence the rule that might makes right, the governors and warlords, mayors and village heads adjusted their orientation one after another.

The Taliban have not 'conquered' Afghanistan in the way that, elsewhere, an army invades a territory. From the Afghan point of view, the Americans in Doha proclaimed them the rulers a second time. If in the end the Afghan soldiers stopped fighting, it was not out of cowardice. In view of the army's immense casualties in the struggle against the Taliban, that accusation is disloyal and immoral. The soldiers stopped fighting because their leadership had been practically dismissed by the headlong Western withdrawal. For the soldiers to oppose the new leadership would have amounted to suicide, and for their officers still more.

The West should have known that, because it had 'conquered' the country in the same way twenty years earlier: not primarily by its own military force, but by winning over the influential parties with money and political promises. Just as one city after another had fallen then like dominos within days into the hands of the Northern Alliance, Afghanistan now fell back into the hands of the Taliban. We can be sure that the dispatches of the German and all other embassies in Kabul predicted exactly this, although the rapidity of the sweep may have surprised them.

It is harmful to our own national interests not to take an interest in the world, to leave the Foreign Ministry and the Defence Ministry to politicians with no international expertise or, as most European heads of government including the German chancellor have done, to weaken Europe steadily so that today it is completely impotent in foreign affairs. In a globalized world it is not realpolitik but idiocy to think the Western community of nations or the European Union could remain uninvolved in troubled regions. Because the result is only that we are dominated by others: mineral resources whose prices we cannot estimate; markets that break away; authoritarian powers that increasingly dictate the reality we live in; whole regions where we can't even go any more; radical political movements gaining strength at home when the feeling of losing autonomy becomes prevalent. There is only one thing Europe will keep hold of in this way, and indeed increase: namely, the problems posed by Afghanistan as a major drug-producing area, a haven for terrorists, and a cause of refugee movements. To keep people from climbing into the boats, we find ourselves in the role of supplicants again, as we were in 2015, and we weaken our negotiating position – only this time we are imploring not just an increasingly authoritarian Turkey but also an Iran that is pursuing nuclear weapons.

Meanwhile the West, by its rash withdrawal from Afghanistan, is tearing down the little that it actually achieved there, namely the spread of an educated middle class striving for individual freedom, which in two, three generations could have become the foundation of a real democracy. The people who are now being flown out are precisely those

Afghanistan would have needed most. And those we leave behind will eventually struggle through to Iran or Pakistan, robbed of all hope and carrying all their remaining possessions in their hands.

And so today, before the eyes of the world, the West is losing an advantage that it has wielded against competing powers over many decades: the promise that its way of life, values and political models represent for the vast majority of people in the world. As for our credibility, we are now in the same league with all the other superpowers, and we can be sure China for one is far superior to us in this regard: no one accuses China of hypocrisy, because it doesn't talk about freedom in the first place. And China is more efficient anyway: right now it is taking over Afghanistan without having deployed a single soldier. If the Soviet tanks withdrawing from Afghanistan stand for the decline of the Soviet Union, the images of Kabul airport symbolize much more directly the West's self-mutilation, not only in a moral sense but still more from a strategic point of view. And even worse will be the photographs that we will not see, because they will not get out.

What is left for us to expect? For one of our politicians to apologize to the Afghan people for the broken promises, even just once, would no doubt be too much. In that case, they could at least apologize to our own soldiers and civilian helpers, whose mission was stripped of all meaning practically overnight.

27

No Programme but Politics

The Chancellorship of Angela Merkel

Die Zeit, Le Monde, 23 September 2021

Angela Merkel has never made a fuss about herself: no private photos, staged holidays, ostentatious appearances, publicly cultivated friendships, and certainly no confessions on the talk-show sets. The most glamour she ever allowed herself was her dresses for the Bayreuth festival, and we may be sure she attended the festival year after year not for the sake of the public attention but because she likes Wagner. Accordingly, she did not sit in the front row but perched four, five or six hours on one of the narrow seats in the middle of the orchestra stalls. Once diagonally behind me in fact, and I noticed her only during the applause. But now, when I think about what impressed me most in the sixteen years of her chancellorship, it is not this or that decision, her negotiating skill, or her self-assertion. It is Angela Merkel the human being. This human being who very rarely appeared in public and yet never hid behind her office. In fact, the one time I talked with her alone, I experienced her as perfectly unpretentious, empathetic, witty, wise.

When I saw her on television after that, in the circle of world leaders, or in Germany among politicians whose personalities seemed to be built of career ladders, I always thought: what a good thing it is that there's definitely a heart beating in at least one breast at that summit meeting! And the fact that Germany was represented by a woman who remained both objective and self-assured in the middle of the boorish men made me as a citizen a little bit proud. At the same time, I was amazed at a charisma that sprang from its own denial, from the unwillingness, and probably the incapacity, to produce big gestures, meaningful glances, profound words and long-term prospects.

Politically, this was a problem, if not *the* problem, of her chancellorship, and not only because of her deficient sense of symbolism. She regularly chose poorly in important staffing matters, whether in Brussels, Berlin or her own party, and the way she greeted the soldiers returning from Afghanistan last spring – namely: not at all – was undignified. Time after time she presented the Bundestag, Germany's parliament and sovereign, with a *fait accompli*, and the European governmental bodies too, by working out resolutions in informal meetings. Perhaps there was sometimes no other way, especially in Brussels. But attempting to reform the institutions where they turned out to be unproductive probably never even crossed her mind.

For, and this is a graver fault than her disdain for democratic pomp, after sixteen years as chancellor, it is hardly possible to associate Angela Merkel with any conviction or agenda except for pragmatism, a basic store of morality, and common sense. And when she did have the verve to venture a controversial position, you could be sure that she would soon assert the opposite. Thus as chancellor she suddenly replaced the liberal economic notions that she had surprisingly presented in her first electoral campaign with solid social-democratic politics, and her pulling out of the pull-out from pulling out of nuclear energy cost Germany many billions of euros.

The list can be continued, not indefinitely, but long enough to give the impression that Angela Merkel was interested less in substance than in what was feasible and also opportune in regard to power politics. In sixteen years, she has not given a single speech on a theme beyond the politics of the day: not on Europe, not on Germany's role in the world, and certainly not on culture; and one can almost understand why. A speech on fundamental principles by Angela Merkel would have seemed like a contradiction in terms. As a result, Germany at the end of her chancellorship is behind in numerous areas: digitalization, education, foreign affairs and security policy, climate protection, transport, infrastructure, European integration; Germany's record in Covid policy too is anything but brilliant compared with that of other European countries. The condition in which she has left the Christian Democratic party is positively dismal. There are reasons for that; it did not just happen.

By understanding politics essentially as problem-solving, Merkel radically narrowed the scope of constructive action, and the will to creative action, to her immediate surroundings and her own presence. This can be seen, for example, in the decision that made her almost a saint in left-wing liberal milieus and gave hope to victims of persecution all over the world: the decision to keep the borders open in September 2015. That was bold; it was profoundly humanitarian; it was, not least, a European impulse. But it was also a 180-degree change of course. For years up to then, it was Germany that had blocked the adoption of a common European refugee policy, ensured that search and rescue in the Mediterranean was stopped, and staunchly opposed a fair distribution of refugees among all the member countries of the European Union. What is more, Angela Merkel herself had blurted out the appalling word *Flüchtlingsbekämpfung*, 'combating refugees', with reference to boat people on the Mediterranean

Sea. And now within one weekend, without parliamentary consultation or public discussion, the same chancellor promulgated the 'welcoming culture'. It is not right-wing populism to point out that, with better preparation and early diplomacy, the decision would not have caused such division in the continent – division going as far as Brexit, which would probably not have been so successful, slim as the majority was that passed the referendum, without the refugee crisis that preceded it.

The history of those hours, the meetings and phone calls, have since been minutely reconstructed. But the chancellor revealed her underlying reason at the time, almost unnoticed, on Anne Will's talk show. 'Up to now we have – and personally I admit it – I have often thought: Syria is far away, Iraq is far away, Afghanistan is far away,' she says near the end of the show, without having been specifically asked, and continues in a surprising, altogether winning self-criticism: 'Now, suddenly, it became apparent that there are people who are running for their lives so that these great distances suddenly shrink down, and they come to us in the EU – that means that we are a part of these conflicts and can no longer separate our foreign from our domestic policy.'

I beg your pardon? The chancellor of the Federal Republic of Germany has a team of foreign policy advisors; her office is served by a ministry with several thousand highly qualified employees who study every single country in the world – and not until the autumn of 2015 did she 'now' and 'suddenly' learn that Germany is affected by the wars in the Middle East and that the refugees set out from their camps in and around Syria months before, after the United Nations refugee agency had cut their rations for lack of funds? Angela Merkel could have found the same words, 'now' and 'suddenly', after the recent disaster in Afghanistan, except that this time it was her own country's citizens and Afghan employees whose peril had gone unnoticed. Once again, the crisis management team met during the weekend. It is not merely coincidence that a great number of dramatic late-night meetings and disruptive decisions occurred during Merkel's term of office. Those who attend only to what lands on their desk are ensuring that their tasks grow steadily more urgent.

The entire history of Merkel's EU policy could be told after the same pattern, from the failed constitution to the financial crisis to the refugee policy; from the authoritarianism and concomitant anti-Semitism of Victor Orbán, whom she tolerated in the European People's Party much too long, to the appointment of second- and third-tier politicians to top European offices, just so that the decision-making power remained with the national leaders; from the refusal even to reply to Emmanuel Macron's proposals for a refounding of Europe to her altogether berserk egoism at the beginning of the pandemic when her government refused to supply masks to Italy, and the chancellor managed in her first televised address to speak about nothing but Germany for fifteen minutes. Time after time, Angela Merkel was busy managing crises – often with remarkable success – that she herself had played a significant part in bringing about through apathy, timidity and nationalistic reflexes.

Now the decline of European foreign and security policy that she supervised for sixteen years has come back to haunt us yet again after Europe was unable even to secure an airport, much less to react to the US agreement with the Taliban by independent diplomatic efforts on the part of the EU. The consequences will not be felt primarily in Washington and New York but in Athens, Berlin and Paris: refugees, terrorism and cheap heroin, with all the accompanying social complications. For the candidates for her succession in the office of chancellor to be asked about nothing but national issues – in the middle of a global pandemic, just weeks after the fall of Kabul, during a profound crisis of the European Union and the Western community of values and amid the global danger of climate change – is the legacy of a policy of reassurance that everything will stay as it has been if we just ensure a modicum of fairness at home, get the vaccination rate up by 10 per cent, and attain Germany's national climate objectives by 2048 instead of 2050. What an illusion!

But can we charge Angela Merkel with provincialism when, after sixteen years in office, she enjoys a worldwide reputation? And what can there have been to criticize about her governance if her potential successors are vying to be as similar to her as possible? The slogan that she posted in her last electoral campaign, 'You Know Me', may have been the epitome of her insubstantiality, and nonetheless – perhaps for that very reason? – the Germans elected her four times in a row. The growing self-righteousness that she has displayed in her last appearances gives us reason to suspect that Merkel herself has become impervious to all criticism, or responds to it as haughtily as she did in her most recent speech in the Bundestag in regard to Afghanistan. And it's true: precisely because I admire her intelligence, her integrity, her sense of duty, I have quarrelled all the more with her politics, and especially with her lack of political vision, for sixteen years. Merkel has apparently satisfied the need of many Germans to be left in peace by a menacing reality. The blame for that is not only hers but at least as much theirs. Customarily, those who dare to institute reforms in Germany – viz. most recently Gerhard Schröder, Merkel's first campaign programme or the Green Party before they began comparing climate protection with a building loan contract – are punished.

And again: the same thing that must be criticized as stagnation and short-sightedness has at the same time a certain quality as poise and self-restraint. It is also part of this chancellor's legacy that politics in Germany today gets along without too much megalomania, machismo and personal defamation – even though the internet has become a massive amplifier for dirt and lies. In any case, the system per se is not called into question every election day. Although in many other Western countries populists, autocrats and Rambos contend for political power, the electoral campaign that is drawing to a close in Germany has been, for all its self-delusion, marked by the candidates' respect for one another. On central social issues, from integration to equality and sexual self-determination to equal educational opportunity, there is a very broad consensus in Germany, from Die Linke to the Free Democrats – in any case, the parliamentary debates are predominantly business-like.

In hindsight, perhaps something like an agenda is discernible precisely where it is not the guiding principles of policy that are concerned but day-to-day cooperation: an agenda that runs from the conference on Islam and the integration summit to the parental allowance, the right to day care, combating anti-Semitism, abolishing obligatory military service, marriage for all, the Welcoming Culture interim and a gender quota in the governing party. And the shift to a more open society that was initiated by the preceding Red–Green coalition government was completed only during Merkel's chancellorship. The considerable acceptance of this change is directly linked to her personally because her pragmatic humanitarianism served as a compass, showing different political camps what the norms are and what is no longer admissible today. It would be no small thing if something similar could one day be said about her successor.

28

Afghanistan? Already a Non-Issue

German Apathy towards the World

Die Zeit, 4 November 2021

On the 26th of August, the last German soldiers came back from Afghanistan. Since then, Germany has had a parliamentary election, public life is returning to normal – for the time being, in spite of rising numbers of new infections – spectators are returning to the stadiums and theatres, one German state after another is celebrating its 75th birthday, the winning parties are negotiating a coalition government while the losers are demolishing one another, and a speed limit on the German autobahn is still nowhere in sight. And Afghanistan? Two months later – did anyone expect otherwise? – it's no longer an issue. The 93,000 German soldiers who served in Afghanistan will just have to deal with the fact that their mission has been made virtually meaningless overnight by the agreement between the United States and the Taliban and by the inaction of European diplomacy. More drastically left to fend for themselves are the thirty-eight million Afghans, of whom a rapidly growing six million are in exile by now. They have to cope with the fact that their country has regressed to its condition of twenty years ago – tyranny, religious extremism, misogyny, contempt for human rights, contempt for culture, contempt for any kind of difference – except that, this time, one more crucial thing is missing: the hope of liberation.

I cannot remember a political event in recent years that upset me as much as the images of people clinging to American aircraft as they took off and falling hundreds of metres to the ground like stones. That is no doubt because of my own memories of the country, so beautiful, so abused, that has been a football to world politics since the invasion of the Soviet Army more than forty years ago. It is also because of my Afghan acquaintances in Germany, whom I have hardly dared look in the eye since August, because every one of them is in despair and uncontainably worried about their relatives, especially their female relatives.

But another reason for the numbed feeling is that, with the failure in Afghanistan, every intercession for democracy all over the world, for the development of civil societies, for liberation, seems to be irrelevant. I have struggled throughout my intellectual life to turn our gaze outwards, for us to see ourselves, in spite of all our love of our respective countries, as citizens of the world. But now the tenor of many commentaries, and especially those in the social media, is this: if our help does so much harm, it would be better for everyone if we didn't intervene anywhere any more. Accordingly, practically nothing was heard during the recent electoral campaigns about our foreign policy, about global responsibility, about international engagement.

Yet what we are now witnessing is not the consequences of the Western mission – its consequences were problematic enough, and I myself have been one of the most vehement critics of the NATO strategy since my first journey through Afghanistan in 2006. What Afghanistan is now undergoing is the immediate effect of our withdrawal. Although its execution was more amateurish and irresponsible than anyone would have thought possible, what has happened is in fact exactly what more than a few groups on the left and the right of the political spectrum had been demanding for years: end the war in Afghanistan! The war has ended, all right. But is anything in Afghanistan the better for it? No – on the contrary; the little good that the Western military intervention had made possible has now been destroyed: women's rights, access to education, a free press, the formation of a civil society, international dialogue, the development of art, literature, music. And the United Nations reports that food supplies to more than half the Afghan population are unsure, and 3.2 million children are already in danger of acute malnutrition. 'Afghanistan is now among the world's worst humanitarian crises, if not the worst,' said David Beasley, the head of the UN's World Food Programme, in late October. 'We are on a countdown to catastrophe.'

Now there is no question of a new military engagement, and so all I can do is to appeal to the world not to forget Afghanistan again. But the words would tie my tongue in knots because I know, as everyone knows, that that is exactly what will happen: Afghanistan will be forgotten again; it practically has been already, two months after the return of our soldiers. Forgotten like Yemen, Ethiopia, Madagascar, Myanmar, Syria, to list just some of the most devastating wars and famines that are not given the least attention in German politics, on German television. But the question that our soldiers' deployment in Afghanistan has raised: that will not go away; it may even be discussed – think of what is going on in Mali – in our crisis meetings and talk shows in the weeks or months to come. I mean the question whether the West, whether Europe, whether Germany's armed forces specifically should intervene in a conflict.

No blood for oil: even the business leaders would probably agree with that, at least in public. But what if a genocide is in progress, women are being raped by the thousands or a dictator uses poison gas against his own population? A state that owes its existence, its freedom, its prosperity to a foreign military intervention should not take the easy way out, after the debacle in Afghanistan, by retreating to the position that it's just not possible to export democracy. The lesson to be learned from both interventions is, rather, that there is no easy answer. The soldiers who go to war not only risk losing their own lives; they also run the risk, even though it is not their intention nor that of their commanders, of further increasing the suffering of a population. But it can also bring death, and in some cases thousands, millions of deaths, when soldiers stay in their barracks.

The invasion of Iraq in 2003 was not only a breach of international law; it was at the same time a disastrous mistake, and we can be grateful – no, we must be grateful – today to Gerhard Schröder for having kept Germany out of that criminal war, against the will of the opposition leader at the time, Angela Merkel. The no-fly zone and the air strikes in Libya in 2011, when millions of insurgents in the eastern part of the country were threatened by the advance of government troops – I admit I was at first unsure whether Germany had been right to abstain, the only Western nation to do so, in the UN Security Council. The German press, the opposition – with the exception of Die Linke – and even his own partners in the coalition government had nothing but criticism for the foreign minister who had brought Germany into a position of isolation. Today we know, and I know, that Guido Westerwelle, may he rest in peace, was right in his doubts about the Libyan opposition and the motives of the West.

A short time later, the disappointment after the lies about Libya had the consequence that no one in the West was willing to protect the rebelling population in Syria against the

Assad regime's barrel bombs and poison gas. Unlike the case of Iraq or Afghanistan, what was proposed was not an intervention by ground troops. The Syrian opposition, which was still in its secular beginnings and led among others by a Christian, Michel Kilo, called for the global community to establish a no-fly zone to stop the military from bombing its own population from the air. After the outbreak of the civil war, there was also the proposal to supply weapons to the Free Syrian Army. Both were rejected; the opposition was left to its fate. Other foreign powers subsequently got involved, in particular Saudi Arabia, Turkey, Russia, Iran; foreign jihadists entered Syria, the so-called Islamic State grew stronger, the democratic revolution increasingly turned into a sectarian conflict, millions of Syrians have lost their homes and hundreds of thousands their lives; the country has been made a rubble heap for decades to come. In hindsight we can say with some certainty that an early engagement by the West in the form of a broad-based diplomatic initiative, massive economic pressure and the use of limited military resources – difficult though it is to calculate consequences – would have prevented such an apocalyptic scenario. Neither would IS have temporarily conquered half the Middle East, nor would the refugee crisis of 2015 have divided Europe to the point of Great Britain's withdrawal from the EU. Yazidis and Christians would not have been driven from their homes; European capitals would not have been afflicted with a series of severe terrorist attacks.

There are many more examples in which our inaction has made a war go on longer, increased the violence – most drastically probably in Rwanda; currently in Yemen. Or remember the siege of Sarajevo, the massacre of Srebrenica, which took place literally before the very eyes of NATO. And there are other countries – I just mentioned two, Iraq and Libya – where it was intervention that led to a conflagration

– or where we utterly failed, as in Afghanistan. Every conflict is different, and often enough the alternatives to be weighed are both wrong because it is too late for the right decision, as it was in 2016 when IS threatened to conquer all of Iraq. At that time, the West quickly decided to provide weapons to the Kurdish army and to support the Shiite popular militias with air reconnaissance, and that was exactly right in that dramatic situation because a genocide against Yazidis and Christians, Kurds and Shiites was imminent. It is unimaginable what would have happened if IS had penetrated Baghdad and the refugee camps in northern Iraq: the mass rapes, beheadings, crucifixions, enslavements.

As I said, these are not debates of the past. Only last May, Robert Habeck caused a commotion by asking whether Ukraine would not have to be supported with weapons in a war against the more powerful Russia, and just this month Germany faces a decision – although it is hardly visible in the news – whether to withdraw the Bundeswehr from Mali. Let us recall: the military mission under French leadership began when jihadists had conquered large parts of the country, up to the legendary city of Timbuktu, subjugating the population, suppressing the local, mystical Islam, and prohibiting practically all aspects of the rich Malian culture. The European military deployment was able to repel the jihadists but failed to achieve essential goals; the country is far from stable, and the recent coup against the civil government this summer did away with the remnants of its democracy. But weren't the goals too ambitious to begin with? And what if Europe leaves Mali to its fate? Will it be Afghanistan all over again? Will the next refugee wave be rolling towards us? Will the next terrorist bombings be planned in Mali? Alas, I don't know. I know only that we have to ask ourselves precisely those questions that make us uncomfortable. We have all had enough of easy answers.

My political socialization took place with the German peace and environmental movement, with the resistance against the nuclear waste repository in Gorleben, and with the sit-in blockade of the Defence Ministry in Hardthöhe. My first car sported a cartoon sticker for many years that shouted 'Fuck the Army'. Since then, however, I have travelled a great deal, and as a reporter I have seen war and violence up close. In Afghanistan, in particular, I know both the view from the Western tanks and the view of the Western tanks, because I have travelled in the country both with NATO and as a civilian. I can no longer say today that we must always oppose foreign deployments. At the same time, I have seen with my own eyes what weapons do, and as a writer I have an allergic reaction when NATO dresses up carpet bombing as 'humanitarian intervention'. War is not humanitarian, and one of the cardinal mistakes of the Western strategy in Afghanistan is that the civilian mission was subordinated from the start to a military logic. NATO, the German army – they are not there to introduce new political systems, consolidate state power and unite war-torn societies. And, nevertheless, the alternative cannot be to look away when ethnic groups are being destroyed, dispossessed, enslaved. The alternative cannot be to refuse all involvement in the world. What is it then? I believe the alternative lies in that broad field between inaction and war that is commonly called politics.

Politics, in this case foreign policy, does not begin with military missions and does not end with talking to dictators, although it includes both of them. Politics means looking for solutions especially when a situation seems hopeless. It means not shrugging your shoulders when basic human rights are violated – freedom, peace, enough to eat, housing – politics means diplomacy, it means dialogue, it means knowledge of the world, it means soul-searching, perseverance, patience.

Politics can also consist of sanctions, threats and, yes, in some cases clearly circumscribed, strictly limited military action. Politics means studying not only our own interests but equally those of others, if only for the simple, selfish reason that we won't be able to preserve our own peace, our own prosperity, if large parts of the world are dominated by hunger and violence. Because the concerns of others soon become our own: in the form of refugees, in the form of attacks, in the form of horrific scenes that we could tolerate only at the cost of our own souls and the civility of our polity.

Not just since this summer – no, for years now we have seen in Germany a dramatic decline in the importance given to foreign policy, both in politics and in the media. Paradoxically, this apathy towards the world seems to have been accelerated yet again by the Afghanistan debacle. The foreign minister used to be, just ten, twenty years ago, the second highest office in the government. Today, it is Heiko Maas. International affairs were absent from the recent electoral campaigns, and now nothing is heard from the current negotiations on a coalition government to indicate much interest in the world across the Mediterranean. Foreign policy is the last thing mentioned in the tentative position paper of the three future governing parties.

At the same time, our lives are more and more dependent on outside factors, down to the most mundane day-to-day activities, and we don't even need to think of the pandemic or climate change or the migration movements which, the United Nations predicts, are going to expand massively in the coming decades. All we need to do is to look at our petrol prices, look at our export volume, look at our phones, whose inner workings require rare earths and lithium. Afghanistan is thought to have some of the world's largest reserves, and that alone is a reason for China not to withdraw from the country. Only the Chinese involvement is not likely to bring the Afghans any closer to freedom. If we do think it's not possible to export democracy, then we should at least take an interest in where our imports come from and where we will be able in future to sell our wares.

The concept of the *Weltbürger*, the citizen of the world, that I referred to above originated in the eighteenth century with Gotthold Ephraim Lessing; it was he who also brought the word cosmopolitanism to the German language. Lessing expressed the same idea very simply in his play *Minna von Barnhelm*: 'It is so sad to be glad all alone.' That is true of individuals, but it is also true of nations, of continents, of humanity. The success of our own country is incredible when you imagine Germany's situation on 8 May 1945: humiliated, bombed flat, morally discredited in the eyes of the world. At least that may give hope to those countries which seem to be in hopeless situations today: the future rarely follows the course we expect, and it can take turns we could never anticipate – for the worse, but sometimes for the better too. In spite of everything that was and is deserving of criticism in Germany, recent German history seems to be just such a miracle. I do not just know this abstractly; I feel it deep in my psyche every time I return from an assignment, and I would like to urge our children, urge every new citizen, to be conscious of this good fortune. No matter what you choose to compare it with, historically, geographically – it is a good country we live in. And yet we can hear, in the line spoken by the eponymous Fräulein in the second act of *Minna von Barnhelm*, not only the sigh, but also the engagement, the vision. It is so sad to be glad all alone.

29

THE PRICE OF JUSTICE

The Disappearance of the Generic Masculine in German

Die Zeit, 4 January 2021

Surah 33, verse 35, begins with a long list:

> See, the loyal men and loyal women,
> The faithful men and faithful women,
> The God-fearing men and God-fearing women,
> The truthful men and truthful women,
> The patient men and patient women,
> The humble men and humble women,
> The charitable men and charitable women,
> The fasting men and fasting women,
> The men and women who guard their modesty,
> The men and women who often think on God –
> God grants them forgiveness and great reward.

The consistent specification of both genders is odd to read or pronounce, and not only in German, but still more for a seventh-century Arabic audience. For, grammatically, the women would not need to be explicitly listed, in Arabic or German, to be included. Why then does the Quran repeat the masculine and feminine forms, over and over again, if the same sense could be expressed more succinctly? The tradition has it that a group of Muslim women had complained to the Prophet that the Quran was addressed mainly to men. Muhammad could have explained to the women, with reference to Arabic grammar, that they are equally meant wherever the Quran mentions the faithful or the God-fearing. But, instead, God revealed to the Prophet the verse cited above, which pointedly lists both genders.

For some time now, in our public language, in the news, in parliamentary debates or in official communiqués, both genders have almost always been explicitly mentioned in references to mixed groups of persons, and, more recently, innovative spellings have been used in German to combine genders explicitly in one word form. And the reason is the same as it was in the seventh century on the Arabian peninsula: where only the masculine form was used, female listeners felt they were not included, or not sufficiently included. As far as I am aware, however, the German language is the only one in which the gender-neutral use of the masculine grammatical form of nouns and pronouns could disappear completely.

The generic masculine has already ceased to be the norm, as is readily observable on reading older books. As late as the 1970s, German women authors – *Autorinnen* – ordinarily called themselves simply authors, *Autoren*, except when they wanted to focus attention on their gender. Today, even where the feminine form is not added to every list, a single woman author would be called *Autorin*, even though the word *Autor* contains no indication of the person's biological gender, and hence encompasses women and men equally. This is certainly an achievement for feminist linguistics, which in the 1980s established the concept of the generic masculine in German as a loan word from English in the first place. In other words, the expression was a controversial one from the beginning – one might say a contentious word intended to call attention to discrimination against women in the language. The likelihood that few Germans were able to translate the adjective 'generic' correctly at the first go placed further strain on the term. In contrast to the biological sense, 'generic' in linguistics does not refer to a person's sex, nor to a person's gender, as most people would probably think off the top of their heads; 'generic' means the opposite: that is, that a grammatical form is used in a generalizing sense, without reference to the attribute of gender. In ordinary language, such a form would more likely be called neutral or genderless. The term 'generic masculine', on the other hand, sounds suspect in itself today.

Recently, cries of desperation have been heard from time to time from German linguists, saying that the grammatical genders must not be confused with biological gender and presenting many words as examples: *die Waise*, the orphan, is grammatically feminine and can be a boy; *der Liebling*, the darling, is grammatically masculine and can be a woman; *das Idol*, the idol, is grammatically neuter but usually a man or a woman; and the female personal pronoun *sie* is also the plural pronoun, in which case it includes both sexes – this is a case of a generic feminine, yet it has not attracted anyone's attention or indignation. In most of the nouns in modern High German, the Munich linguist Olav Hackstein wrote recently in the *Frankfurter Allgemeine Zeitung*, the masculine gender denotes individual entities, as in *der Fluß*, river, stream or flow; the so-called feminine gender is normally reserved for collective and abstract nouns, such as *die Flut*, flood, deluge or high tide, or *die Überschwemmung*, flood, inundation or submersion. Finally, the neuter gender can designate indefinite masses, as in *das Wasser*, water. The grammatical genders have no more to do with biological gender than the accusative case with the accusation after which it is named (Latin *accusare*, blame, accuse). They have not lost an association with biological gender in the course of time; quite the opposite: the function which the different categories of nouns has always had was not associated with different genders, as an easy way to distinguish them, until grammar became an object of study.

The opposing arguments are no doubt well known by now, and they cannot be dismissed out of hand either. For, indeed, language is never neutral; it always reflects social and political conditions. Thus the notion of a divine being, which was often connoted as female in the early history of religion, has for thousands of years been overlaid with masculine pronouns and attributes, and that is of course not an act of Providence but the expression of a patriarchal order that has taken shape all over the world. Most importantly, however, language is not a static system that is independent of its speakers. It is not only speaking, it is also hearing, and if it is heard differently today, with particular sensitivity to gender inequality for example, the language changes. From the Quran we learn that Arab women listeners perceived the generic masculine as excluding them as early as the seventh century; it should not surprise us that more recent studies show still more clearly that women do not feel they are addressed in the same way as men where nouns are used only in the masculine – in job postings, for example.

No matter how often a linguist points out that a word such as *Leser*, readers, is a generic term and hence one would need to say *männliche Leser*, male readers, when the intended meaning is exclusively men – from the moment no one hears the women readers in the word *Leser* any more, the linguist's opinion must be consigned to historical linguistics. The editors of Germany's dictionary of record, the Duden, have already anticipated that moment and officially done away with the generic masculine: thus *ein Mieter* is now exclusively 'a male person who has hired something'. And yet I myself continue to use words such as *Leser* and *Hörer* (listeners) as gender-neutral – that is, unlike today's newsreaders, I do not append the feminine form every time. Why?

Let me return once more to the word God: as much as it is and has been suppressed, the femininity of God has been conserved in the religions in one way or another: in mysticism, in popular piety, and especially in art. This is the case even in monotheism, which does not admit male and female divinities, nor androgynous divine beings, as Hinduism does. Wisdom, Sophia, is revered in the Bible as a person descended from God, but independent – and female, His bride; and in rabbinic Judaism and the Kabbalah, God Himself has feminine traits in the form of the *shekhinah*, His 'indwelling' on Earth. Christianity, which sees God as incarnated in a man, also sanctifies the Mother of God in the Orthodox and Catholic churches: since C. G. Jung, analytical psychology has rightly recognized the veneration of Mary as a means by which popular piety compensates for the Church's masculine conception of God. In Islam, the most important and most frequently occurring attribute of God, *raḥma*, or mercy, has clearly feminine connotations; the word itself is derived from *raḥim*, womb. Islamic mysticism, which has developed to a significant degree through the encounter with the Asian religions, ascribes both male and female attributes to God. But if God is both man and woman, then so are human beings – all human beings. Because the divine reality is reflected in every person.

Naturally I am not referring to a biological reality, although, as we know, there are children whose sex is not clearly identifiable. All cultures have developed an understanding of the fact that the human psyche is composed of different and in part contradictory elements which are associated more with masculinity or more with femininity. The ideal has always been to balance the two forces and make them productively complement each other, as for example the yin and yang of Chinese philosophy or animus and anima in Jung's analytical psychology. This duality of the soul is reflected in the paradoxical experience of the Divine as awe-inspiring and attractive at once: *mysterium tremendum* and *mysterium fascinosum* in Rudolf Otto; the majesty and beauty of God in Islam; contraction and expansion in mysticism; inhalation and exhalation in Goethe.

For that reason, I experience the opening and broadening of sexual determinations which began with feminism, and is now propagated throughout the Western world by the queer movement, not only as a social emancipation. In the diverse transitions, intersections and ambiguities there is – although it is not apparent or does not seem urgent to all parties – a fundamental truth of religious psychology and anthropology. I cannot imagine, by the way, biased though I admittedly am, that anyone in the world has benefited more from the women's movement than myself. For if I had been born only a generation earlier, I would have been deprived of the greatest blessing of my life: namely, the privilege of bringing up my two children as an equally participating father, with all the tenderness and obligations, cares and happiness of the motherliness that every human being has inside them, whether man or woman. Our fathers spent far less time with their children, and my father for one laughed at me in the beginning when I came in the door carrying the baby slung in front of my stomach, or when he found me changing nappies; but towards the end of his life he deeply regretted the fact that such closeness had been unthinkable for a man of his generation, both in Iran and in Germany.

We are not unambiguous, any of us, neither ethnically nor culturally, neither psychologically nor sexually, and an uncompromising, exclusive masculinity has proved to be toxic time after time, both in the history of the world and in the history of religion. Significantly, Theodor W. Adorno made a utopian motif not of identity – that is, an entity's oneness with the qualities externally ascribed to it – but of the non-identical: that is, where something or someone is not equal to what is conceivable of it, her, him. Identity politics, which determines certain sexual or ethnic characteristics of a person and assigns them to a supposedly homogeneous group, has always been terror and has remained so in its present-day forms, whether left or right, whether religious or nationalist, whether backward-looking or intended as emancipatory, and often enough it leads to physical violence.

But language categorizes: that is its nature as a system of symbols; that is, it assigns the experiential world, which is diverse, ambiguous, and ultimately infinitely complex, to a necessarily limited number of terms. Language says 'love', although everyone knows that the word alone says nothing because what it signifies to can be so different, extending even to its complete opposite. Language says 'root', and in so doing applies a single term not only to a practically incomprehensible biological diversity but also figuratively to all kinds of other meanings. Language divides one thing from another: a chair from a table, intellect from emotion, grief from happiness – although we know from physics, from psychology and certainly from mysticism that everything is connected with everything else through an endless web of relationships. Language is – no, it must be – pragmatic, otherwise there could be no appointments, no social organization, no theories and no poker nights. Language says 'man' and 'woman', although all the spiritual teachings offer, in one way or another, the wisdom that no aspect of human nature, least of all our sexuality, fits into a rigid dichotomy of genders. Thus language, by its necessary simplification, constantly runs the risk of reducing complexity, of solidifying conditions, of being mistaken for biological reality. It entails the risk of squeezing all those who are subsumed under a given attribution – let us say, all Jews, all Germans, all Blacks . . . gays, Asians, men, women, or transsexuals – into a single identity.

No language in the world always names all the genders when it refers to a mixed group of persons – that would be too laborious for everyday language and too cumbersome for poetry. And languages don't need to list them all, because what they mean is not encoded one-to-one in what they say. Languages tend, in Olav Hackstein's phrase, to be 'economical systems of communication', characterized by implication: every listener understands what is meant even though it is not said explicitly. In other words, language functions in no small degree by what the speaker doesn't say, but the listeners think, along with the speaker. Language is too pragmatic in its purpose and all too limited in its means to deal in explicit unambiguous signifiers.

This is the reason, in addition to all the linguistic and aesthetic reasons, why I perceive explicitly gender-inclusive German – the use of an asterisk or a colon to indicate the human genders that cannot be expressed in grammatical genders, i.e. *Leser*innen* or *Leser:innen* for 'readers' – not as emancipating but as an intellectual and political regression. Gender attributions do not fit into two categories, but they do not fit into twenty-seven either. To think we could do justice to each person all the time by means of language is not only a misunderstanding of the nature of language; it also introduces an assignment of identity where there was none before. To express the diversity, the ambiguity, the contradictions of human nature, and the perceptions of it, is not the purpose of our everyday language; much less is it the duty of any official or academic body: that is the task, and in fact the purpose, of literature, music, art: an impossible task which they achieve again and again, in the most astounding ways. An author such as Proust is able to encompass all the nuances and paradoxes of human desire in just a single page. Kleist equates love and hate; Beckett finds words for speechlessness; Simone Weil thinks of God and nothingness at the same time. Literature does not describe exhaustively what everyday language is able to phrase concisely. On the contrary, it purposely creates lacunae where the reader's imagination is drawn into the work.

I happen to know two languages, Persian and English, in which nouns have no grammatical gender. Do these languages offer the writer an advantage? It is a fallacy that linguistic equality between the sexes must result in real social equality – otherwise things would be different in Turkey and Iran. Language is an expression of reality, including social reality and social inequality as the case may be, but it is not an instrument to change reality. Language changes automatically as the reality changes, except in totalitarian systems.

For literature, however, the ambiguity of gender attribution is an enormous advantage. The homoerotic poetry of Persia, for example, draws on the fact that it can leave undetermined whether a given lover is male or female. Although we know from the biographical literature that Rumi's great love poems were addressed to a man (as were most of Shakespeare's sonnets, for that matter), his readers and the political authorities have pretended for centuries, down to present-day Iran, that they speak to a woman. And Rumi certainly intended his poems to have precisely this universal sense: that love was not made for a specific combination of sexes – especially since he was singing about not just earthly love but at the same time the love between God and human beings, between Creator and creatures.

I experienced something comparable when, at fifteen or sixteen, I first heard Rio Reiser's records. I hadn't the slightest idea that Rio Reiser was gay and that his lyrics, his longing, his desire referred to a man. In the West German town of Siegen in the early 1980s there were no gays, no lesbians – for young people like me, homosexuality was not illicit; it was simply non-existent. Only in hindsight can I guess who among my classmates had different sexual preferences from most others, and I can imagine how they must have suffered under the taboo. When I found out, near the end of my school years, that none other than my favourite German rock singer loved a man, something in my head went – I remember it vividly – click: man, woman, doesn't matter, I thought – the love that Rio Reiser is singing of can't be wrong. May he rest in peace.

Now, the second-person *du*, 'you', that Rio Reiser addressed to his love has no gender. When I write about love in the third person in a novel, on the other hand, I occasionally curse German grammar, because it forces me to reveal a lover's gender: write either *der Geliebte*, masculine, or *die Geliebte*, feminine. It would leave much more room for the readers' imagination if they didn't know in which direction the first-person narrator's love was sprouting. If the mere circumstance of a man imagining a woman's point of view has become offensive today, that should be all the more motivation to insist on the non-identical that is inherent in every artistic act.

At the same time, the German language permits nuances that would not be possible in English or Persian. I can make gender attributions visible, but thanks to the generic masculine I can also make them disappear where they are not significant. If for example I send an e-mail to my friends to invite them to my birthday party, then I purposely do not address them as *Freundinnen und Freunde*, friends (female) and friends (male). The word *Freundin*, sent by a man, would have an undesirable, ultimately erotic connotation – the same word serves to signify girlfriend – which would seem to me out of place in the context of a birthday invitation. If, on the other hand, as a lecturer I write an e-mail to my students, I consistently address them as *liebe Studenten und Studentinnen*, dear students (male) and students (female) – even though the female students are not attending my seminar in their capacity as women. No one would infer from my salutation that their gender particularly interests me; the reason for it is rather the opposite. Women students today might take it as an affront or an exclusion if I insisted on the generic masculine. Because I cannot bring myself to substitute the now customary but semantically incorrect and, moreover, ugly participle *Studierende*, those who are studying, it is necessary to mention both sexes. To address the women students explicitly as *Studentinnen*, even though they would otherwise be semantically included in *Studenten*, is to me both a natural act of politeness and one that makes our life more pleasant.

Language, culture, civilization – they do not consist merely of necessities. They also consist of that which, by strict rules, would be superfluous. Poetry especially is made by breaking the rules. The German language, and probably all languages that have grammatical gender, permit emphases, overtones and many kinds of deviations from the grammatical norm which I can no longer imagine doing without in my literary writing. To be able, but not required, to feminize a noun, depending on the context, also broadens the variabilities of melody and rhythm; it allows assonances where the roots of several words are different.

But the feminine ending – no matter how I vary its use – is not just a literary resource. It is also a semantic asset. To stick with day-to-day language: I can refer to a woman colleague as the most important author – *der bedeutendste Autor* – in contemporary German literature. But I can also call her *die bedeutendste Autorin*, the most important woman author, in contemporary German literature. Both are possible, but the meaning is different, obviously. The generic masculine permits a more concise and at the same time precise expression; without it, my superlative would have to refer to my colleague as *die bedeutendste aller Autoren und Autorinnen* – the most important of all authors (male) and authors (female) in contemporary German literature. But language, the language of our daily communication, is pragmatic, and therefore the evolution of language generally tends to simplify. For that reason, I do not think that explicitly gender-inclusive German will prevail in the spoken language. Not only does it lack acceptance outside of a limited milieu which, contrary to its self-perception, is extraordinarily homogeneous; but the gender-inclusive forms are also simply too cumbersome, complicated and unmusical to catch on in day-to-day life, much less in the literary language. At most, the asterisk may hold its ground in bureaucratic German, and the glottal stop that marks its presence in speech may become a distinguishing mark of the educated, socially privileged classes.

What will probably disappear from the German language, however, is the generic masculine. As I said, language is not the motor but the expression of social developments, and linguistic equality between the sexes seems to be a widely shared concern. As a writer, I can regret the loss; I can point out that precisely the renunciation of a gender-neutral use of words reinforces the sexualization of the language; I can oppose the disappearance of the generic masculine; but, at the same time, of course I want to avoid my language being perceived as impolite or associated with a socially conservative message that affirms antiquated gender roles. If language is not just speaking but also hearing, then I cannot ignore the fact that younger listeners especially – female listeners explicitly included – no longer recognize the generic masculine because their German teachers do not teach it. All that I can do, then, is hope that the gender-neutral use of masculine nouns and pronouns will not yet, at least in my lifetime, be misunderstood as a provocation and its sense thus reversed. When a grammatically masculine form no longer elides the biological gender but instead overemphasizes it, then the generic masculine will be definitively dead.

But does not the Quran already repudiate the generic masculine? No, it ignores it in a specific context for a specific purpose in the verse cited, and in many others which are rightly highlighted by feminist exegesis. As far as we know, the Quran is the earliest of all Arabic texts to address women directly, and the tradition tells of male listeners who were exceedingly annoyed by this. In general, though – that is, where there is no intentional emphasis on the listeners' gender – the Quran lets the masculine form suffice. In other words: as in any other poetic work, breaking the rule presupposes that the rule exists.

In his *Meccan Revelations*, the great mystic Muhyiddin Ibn Arabi lists the spiritual qualities of the 'perfect person', the *insān kāmil*. In the style of Surah 33, verse 35, quoted above, he adds after every single quality the identical adjunct *mina r-rijāl wa-n-nisā*: 'among the men and among the women'. Semantically, this is redundant: the word for 'person', *insān*, although grammatically masculine, includes both sexes in Arabic. Nevertheless, it is beautiful, and socially necessary, for Ibn Arabi to add the phrase, then as now. Only in a society where equality had been achieved would it no longer be necessary to deviate from the generic masculine. Its disappearance, conversely, does not advance equality an inch.

30

War as a Means of Politics

After Vladimir Putin's Announcement of a Russian Troop Deployment to Donbas

Die Zeit, 24 February 2022

With Vladimir Putin's announcement that Russian troops would be deployed to Luhansk and Donetsk, war has definitively become a means of politics in Europe once more – regardless of whether Russia actually invades Ukraine by the time this newspaper is issued, or will invade in the future. Because now even a diplomatic solution, whatever it might look like, would be the result of Russia's massive military pressure, and hence a victory for Putin. And his triumph might turn out to be still greater if the invasion does not occur, or if it is limited to the regions already practically occupied. Because then Moscow could reiterate its constant claims that its soldiers were assembled for a defensive exercise and had not threatened Ukraine at any time. The American president Biden would then have falsely predicted the day of the attack several times and would appear as hysterical, a liar and the real warmonger – and not only to the Russian public. No, the constantly growing part of the Western population who fear Russia less than globalization and liberal democracy would also have another reason to see Putin as the example of a strong, dominant leader – and, with the population, those Western politicians who make the case for nationalism, whether Trump, Zemmour and Orbán on the right, or Mélenchon, Grillo and Wagenknecht on the left. No one would talk about the Russian annexation of Crimea, the annexation of Donbas or Lukashenko's tyranny any more, and it would be likewise clear that Ukraine has no prospects in Europe. Other countries would think hard about whether they want to follow the West, or whether they hadn't better try to align with Moscow or Beijing. Democratic revolutionary movements would be left on their own to an even greater degree. Shrewdly used, war is sometimes a very efficient instrument of politics, I am sad to say.

After the end of the Soviet Union, the danger of a military conflict between the superpowers seemed to have been averted – for who would make war on whom if there was only one superpower left? Of course weapons were still used, populations expelled, people massacred, but it was no longer proxies fighting one another as it had been during the Cold War. The American interventions in Kuwait, in the Balkans, in Somalia in the nineties, and in Afghanistan in 2001 were not components of any long-term plan; in each case, Washington was directly reacting to an occupation, an impending genocide or a terrorist attack. The reasons were not simply made up; their legitimacy, even where it was not universally accepted and ratified by a UN resolution, was not deniable out of hand. So when did military force become a means of enforcing strategic and economic interests in global politics? In hindsight, it is apparent that it began in 2003 with the United States' invasion of Iraq.

The official reasons – the nuclear threat of Saddam Hussein, his alleged support of jihadism, the establishment of a democracy – were all unconvincing even before the war began, and they soon turned out to be lies. In the rather blunt phrases of the neo-conservative strategists, America wanted to expand its dominance, secure access to Iraqi oil, topple a formerly allied, now undesirable ruler, and install a submissive regime between its partner Israel and its enemy Iran. Furthermore, the Bush administration left little doubt that, after the conquest of Baghdad, Tehran would be the next target, so that the United States would dominate the entire region from Kabul to Jeddah and from Karachi to Cairo, with its abundance of oil and minerals. In fact, the resources for a hybrid war against the Islamic Republic under George W. Bush had already been allocated and deployed.

Of course, the neo-conservative vision of a liberal, America-friendly Middle East failed spectacularly. Instead of American influence expanding from Baghdad to Iran, Iraq fell into the sphere of influence of the Islamic Republic, for which the American invasion proved rejuvenating. And, as if that were not failure enough, Tehran subsequently expanded its influence tremendously in Syria and Lebanon too: thus George W. Bush and Tony Blair not only plunged Iraq into chaos but, at the same time, delivered the means for Iran's leader of the revolution, Khamenei, and the Revolutionary Guards to consolidate their rule, in spite of the rebellious population and the dire economic situation – and the Iranian prisons are full of political prisoners today.

And that is still not all: by starting another war two years after the fall of the Taliban, Bush Jr and Blair gave away the victory in Afghanistan that had already seemed certain. I remember well a conversation with two British brigadier generals at the headquarters of the NATO troops in Kabul in 2006: they described to me the negative consequence of the Iraq War for the mission in Afghanistan. Unlike the Iraq War, the war in Afghanistan was winnable, they assured me, but it would require the willingness to commit sufficient resources – and not just military resources but, most importantly, political support, unwavering developmental aid, and broad-based investments in infrastructure and education. The financial and military resources that America had been deploying in Iraq since 2003 had been lacking since then for the pacification and economic development of Afghanistan. In comparison with the legacy of Bush Jr, Donald Trump's presidency looks almost harmless, at least as far as foreign policy is concerned.

Today, the United States is further away than ever from being a force for good fighting evil all over the world. The world is not more peaceful, nor more free, as a result. Because wherever the US withdraws, it abandons the field to other players. China is able to expand its sphere of influence, country by country, almost without the use of physical force, simply by its economic power and its strategic intelligence. Russia, on the other hand, lacking the economic and technological incentives, is significantly more heavy-handed. As early as 2016 in Syria, it demonstrated to a surprised global public how intervention can succeed: with far fewer military means than America deploys, just as many lies, and still greater ruthlessness.

In the search for reasons for success and failure in the Middle East, a look at recent history is helpful: after the demise of the Soviet Union and the rapid successes in the previous Gulf War and in Afghanistan, America was euphoric when it invaded Iraq. The Red Army meanwhile, after its defeat in the Hindu Kush, was still afraid when it landed in Syria. In addition, the Kremlin must have studied precisely how the United States had succumbed to its own hubris, first in Iraq, then gradually in Afghanistan, and finally, in 2011, in Libya too. Thus realism and the strict limitation to its own objectives saved Russia from the quagmire that President Obama had predicted in the case of an intervention in Syria.

Encouraged by its unexpected success, and yet keeping a cool head, Russia has once again risen to the role of an imperial power in other parts of the world as well – in Latin America, in Africa and, first and foremost of course, in the territories it had lost at the fall of the Soviet Union. The intervention in Syria preceded the annexation of Crimea and the invasion of the Donbas, which the West was hardly able to oppose with more than diplomatic entreaties. Actually, war had already returned to Europe at that point, in 2014, only we largely ignored it then. Germany in particular really began to expand its natural gas business with Russia after that, which was hardly advantageous for the Minsk negotiations. And Europe? Notoriously, the answer has long been: Oh. Instead of acting as the strong, self-assured actor with a constant commitment to its values, a role it could claim by virtue of its size and economic power, the European Union, with its inadequate institutional structures and the egoism of its national leaders, remains paralysed in regard to foreign policy – by the very same toxin that Moscow has been cooking up through its xenophobic campaigns and support for nationalist parties.

Will there be a hot war? Those who still comfort themselves that Putin's cost–benefit calculation will stop him from invading Ukraine should read the disturbing but probably realistic essay that Liana Fix and Michael Kimmage published a few days ago in the journal *Foreign Affairs*: in spite of all the anticipated difficulties and sanctions, the intervention could yet prove realpolitically more profitable than those before in the Donbas, in Crimea, in the Caucasus, and in Syria.

But a Russian victory in Ukraine, even if it is initially less triumphant than the American victory in Baghdad, would change Europe more profoundly than any other event since the fall of the Berlin Wall. Then the New World Order would be rung in not just in the Middle East or on the Black Sea – no, it would have found its way to the middle of

Europe. NATO would have been made a fool of; the next military conflict would be almost guaranteed. Especially for a country such as Germany, which lives on its exports and hence depends on stable conditions, and at the same time would prefer to take a step backwards when there is something to be sorted out somewhere in the world, it would be the end of easy living.

Interestingly, the fronts in German debates run perpendicular to the political camps, and there are genuine arguments on both sides: yes, Russian fears must be taken seriously, although the Kremlin is certainly instrumentalizing and stoking them, but they are deeply rooted in the people's collective consciousness for obvious reasons. And if we picture the mistrust that prevails in Russia after the West did not stand by the announcement of the German foreign minister Hans-Dietrich Genscher that NATO would not be enlarged eastwards, that does not make us apologists for Putin; it is only what in military jargon would be called civil reconnaissance. Not to have integrated Russia in the European security architecture and NATO in the 1990s remains a mistake with far-reaching consequences. The impression of having been deceived and rejected was manifested in almost every sentence of Putin's agitated speech that shocked the West on Monday. It would be disastrous to think it expressed only the private wrath of a single politician who longs to be counted among the world's great leaders. Putin touches on a feeling that happens to exist in parts of the Russian population, whether it is reasonable or not. That makes his volley of abuse so dangerous.

But it is also true that Moscow too has broken a promise, one which was written in a treaty in 1994, in fact, when Ukraine gave up its atomic arsenal: the promise to respect Ukraine's sovereignty and its existing borders. Those who still think today that the Russian threat should be met merely with warnings or undetermined sanctions are encouraging an escalation. For then, as before in Chechnya, Abkhazia, Ossetia, Syria and eastern Ukraine, there would be no penalty for war. That is why Germany does horrible damage to its credibility when, after supplying four billion euros' worth of arms to Egypt's brutal dictator Abdel al-Sisi just in the past year, it can spare only five thousand helmets for democratic Ukraine in the face of a substantial threat. Berlin is even preventing Estonia from transferring supplies it acquired from the East German army to Kyiv. Yes, it is possible to oppose German weapons exports and, certainly, to defend that opposition on grounds of German history. However, we should then be logical and accept the economic costs to Germany instead of extending our hand only where it does not endanger gas imports.

Ukraine lacks many things, but alternatives to German weapons are probably not one of them. If Berlin cannot bring itself to support Ukraine militarily, it could show all the more diplomatic fortitude. How about advocating now – I mean now, as a reaction to Putin's speech, alongside the sanctions already announced – that Brussels begins the procedure to admit Ukraine to the European Union? If the offer also makes allowances for Ukraine's economic ties to Russia instead of creating a hard eastern border that cuts off the flow of goods, the message would be clear that bringing Kyiv closer to Europe is not about military or economic supremacy but about those democratic values that people died for in the Maidan. After all, membership in NATO, as all the parties know, will remain unrealistic for the foreseeable future anyway. The prospect of belonging to the EU, on the other hand, would be a signal that Ukraine is not a source of danger – or only that danger to authoritarian regimes that the much greater appeal of free societies poses.

31

THROUGH THE NIGHT

Ukraine at War
Die Zeit, 5 May 2022

No place in Kyiv is as dark at night as the railway station. That is, it is dark all over the city, but while the streets appear deserted because of the curfew, crowds swarm around the trains and, when you stumble over someone's luggage, the lack of light jumps out at you, almost like a flash. Only the silhouettes of the people are discernible, and sometimes the faces, lit by the glow of smartphone screens. Why do they speak so softly? Might the people firing rockets from far away not only see lights but also hear voices? Or is the darkness casting a gloom over their spirits as well? Shining my flashlight alternately at the train and the platform, I look for my carriage.

In the daytime, Kyiv seems almost like a normal city again – although one in which every day is Sunday. Only a few shops are open; nevertheless, a surprising number of cars roll along the streets, and even the first joggers are out and about. The sirens, which don't whine at all on some days, then do again at short intervals, hardly seem to draw any attention – at least, no one quickens their pace. Even I have grown accustomed to the air-raid alarms surprisingly quickly. Since the first night, when I hurried with the other guests to the lobby of my hotel in Lviv, I have begun to take reassurance from the improbability of a rocket landing right on top of me. In the middle and west of the country, the probability is so low by now that more normality is returning day by day. At the station, I realize that the war is threatening to become normal in Ukraine. It takes forever for the train to start, as all the trains seem to run late, two, three or seven hours, without anyone complaining; never mind as long as you get away. Where the city ends, when the open countryside begins, I can only guess behind the window of the sleeper, because everything looks the same in the blackness.

The day before yesterday, my travelling companion Katya Lachina and I were walking through Bucha, where time now will always be divided into a before and an after, and the first thing that surprised us was how fast we got there: in just thirty, forty minutes; that is how close the horror had come to Kyiv. Since the mass graves have been dug and the transmitter trucks have gone, something like a day-to-day routine has returned, even in the ruins: the routine of food distribution, the routine of clearing rubble, the routine of burying the bodies that are still being found. Not all of them died by bullets, shells or bombs. Many of the inhabitants succumbed during the occupation because they fell sick, in sub-zero temperatures week after week without electricity, without heat, without clean water; with only their own food supplies and the constant fear. Others, especially older people, died of a shock or a heart attack right at the beginning. And then some people had already died before the war, and were lying in the morgue when the power was cut off – what to do? While it was still possible, they were taken to other towns where the refrigeration still worked, but which body was taken where? There was hardly time to record that properly. Now that the mass graves have been filled in again, bodies are being brought back to Bucha every day to be identified.

A note behind the windscreen that says 'Cargo 200' indicates what is in the vehicles. That is the transport code for the remains of the fallen, carried over from the Soviet war in Afghanistan.

The relatives looked mutely at two delivery vans parked back to back, while the long, black plastic sacks were lifted from one cargo space to the other. Because it was raining, two helpers held up umbrellas, while a third argued with the foreign photographers who would not be kept away. So hard to preserve the dignity of the dead in some way when there are so many of them, and then along come these vultures too, members of my own profession. After the sacks have been briefly opened for identification, the autopsy follows, which, like everything else apparently during these weeks, is performed by volunteers – volunteer doctors in this case. In their wrinkled white full-body suits, they smoked a cigarette in front of the morgue before pulling their air filters over their faces again. Around the back of the building, the bodies already autopsied lie side by side on steel bunks, waiting to be buried at last.

The first field, with 117 anonymously buried bodies, was found behind St Andrew's Church, and so we spoke to the priest there, who was loading supplies into a minivan. His name was Andrew, he introduced himself; yes, just like that of his church; to judge by his facial expression, others before me had also remarked on the shared name. He had no more than a minute and a half to spare, he said, yet he put down the carton he was carrying when I asked what the hardest moment for his congregation had been. The hardest thing was not the sight of the bodies, he said. The hardest thing for the relatives was always seeing the face, even when they were only shown a photograph.

And what did the relatives ask you? I asked.

They asked me why God permitted it.

And what did you answer?

I answered that we cannot hold God responsible for something human beings have to answer for. God did not kill; people killed. God did not bless the war; Kyrill blessed the war.

But isn't Kyrill still the patriarch to most of the Christians in Ukraine?

The Ukrainians can no longer do otherwise than to break away from the Russian Orthodox Church. And by that I mean not just my parish; I mean all of us. It is a painful process, but it has become unavoidable with this war. We must believe in a loving God.

Father Andrew held out in Bucha during the entire time of the occupation, but rarely dared leave the church. The other inhabitants had also stayed in their cellars and lived on their provisions, he said. For that reason they had hardly encountered the Russian soldiers at first. Not even in the church? The Russians didn't seem to feel like praying, the priest answers: how could a person pray who was murdering, torturing or raping? I asked whether the soldiers had been so brutal right from the beginning. No, the real atrocities had taken place in the last week, two weeks before the withdrawal. Father Andrew can only speculate about the reasons: the frustration of having to turn back so close to Kyiv, the alcohol, the boredom – or maybe an order. But, since then, no one here sees the Russians as a brother nation any more.

A few kilometres further on, in Borodianka, we looked into a crater that gaped between two blocks of flats. Where the hole was, there had also been a housing block, we learned. Forty-five people were buried under it when the rocket hit. The rubble had already been removed, but a few men were still digging in the ground. What were they looking for, we asked. For the internet cable, they answered. There is still no electricity, running water, no heating, but they are already trying to find their connection to the world again.

One of the men offers to show us the building that the occupiers used as their headquarters. His home is practically next door to it. He leads us across a football pitch to a playground whose equipment seems to date from Soviet times, like the prefab housing blocks around it. There he points to a shed where the male inhabitants were interrogated. Yes, he too was made to kneel and was asked, with a rifle pointed at his forehead, which of his neighbours belonged to the Banderites. The Russian media call the alleged Nazis from which they are liberating Ukraine by the name of the twentieth-century nationalist politician Stepan Bandera. Many men were also maltreated; our guide, fortunately, was not. He insisted he didn't know any Banderites. The men who were shot are evidently those whom the soldiers did not believe.

What do you think today about the Russians, I ask: do you think you'll be able to live in peace with them again some day?

I'm practically a Russian myself, the man answers; almost all my ancestors are from Russia; I speak the same language; those were people like us.

Back in Kyiv, I ask the religious scholar Ihor Kozlovsky whether the close connections between Russians and Ukrainians could be a cause of the conflict, as in so many wars in the world. Kozlovsky, one of the most respected scholars in the country, is from Donetsk, where he was held captive and tortured for two years by pro-Russian separatists before being released in late 2017 in a prisoner exchange. Closeness is relative, Kozlovsky answered; the closer you look, the more differences you notice. Then he launched into a half-hour lecture on the tangled and tense web of relationships between the two nations.

And will this war now be the definitive rupture?

Yes, this will be the rupture, a complete separation. A great number of families are currently breaking apart too.

Many Ukrainians have told me about such divisions: about the horror when they talked on the telephone with relatives in Russia during the air raids. There are no missiles, they were told, or if there are missiles they are Ukrainian, or if they are Russian missiles, then only to liberate Ukraine from the Nazis. And so on. After that, they say, they are not so eager to phone Russia, and, when they do, they talk only about superficial topics.

This war is not about ethnicity, said Kozlovsky; nor is it about territory, about language. It is about values. We do not want to live like them. We do not want a president who is always the same. Ukraine is a European country which has always been oriented towards the West, much more so than Russia. We want to belong to Europe again.

I asked whether Ukraine is not denying an important part of its own history, its own identity, if it turns away from Russia, breaks off the relationship with the Russian intellectual world, and treats Russian civilization only as something foreign and hegemonic. After all, any nationalism ultimately leads to ignorance of one's own culture, which is never pure and homogeneous. That is true, Kozlovsky answered, but now the time has come for a greater awareness of what is Ukrainian, the time to distinguish and delimit. More and more people, he said, are beginning to speak Ukrainian instead of Russian in day-to-day life, and even the Russian Orthodox Church in Ukraine has stopped including the patriarch of Moscow in its prayers – after a thousand years. Vladimir Putin wanted to annihilate Ukraine; instead, to put it dramatically, he created Ukraine. No other event, Kozlovsky said, has contributed so much to building the Ukrainian nation as this war.

The next day we went to Chernihiv, the major city north of Kyiv that was besieged for five weeks. Because the bridges of the main roads were demolished ahead of the invading Russians, and there are numerous checkpoints to be crossed on the side roads, the 150 kilometres take four to five hours. But this takes you through the villages that were under Russian occupation, through landscapes dotted with ruins, past abandoned farms. Although we heard nothing about orgies of violence like those in Bucha, the people we spoke to along the way were still under the shock of the forty-five days they had spent mostly in their cellars. Some told us about the looting, and an old woman railed that the Russians were worse than the Germans, who had at least asked for the food they took. Are there still inhabitants who still feel, here, so close to the borders of Russia and Belarus, a part of the Russian hemisphere? No doubt they exist, said a priest who had only contempt for the Moscow patriarch, but even they realized that this is not a very good time to proclaim their attachment to Russia. How many in his parish would still oppose joining the Orthodox Church of Ukraine is therefore hard to estimate, he said: maybe 20 per cent, maybe 30.

Not so few after all, I said.

Yes, but the Ukrainian Orthodox Church is only thirty years old. That's practically nothing.

In almost all the villages, we saw station wagons, vans or trucks from which food, clothes and necessities were being distributed. As far as I was able to find out, they had all been stocked and sent by private initiatives – here a neighbourhood centre, there a biathlon club or a boy scout troop. The first time I travelled in Ukraine, in 2016, I did not have the impression at all that people were particularly interested in the war in the Donbas. Many of the Ukrainian soldiers there felt not only betrayed by their own government but also forgotten by society. The inferior equipment, the battered weapons, the bad pay – it took a great deal of patriotism for them to risk their lives in the trenches. Now, not only have hundreds of thousands of men volunteered – no, the whole country seems to be involved in distributing aid, and that may be an indication of the real reason why Russia's progress is so laborious in this war: on one side an army is fighting; on the other, a nation.

Significantly, I hear practically nothing in my conversations about Volodymyr Zelenskyy, the Ukrainian president who is being celebrated as a hero in the West. Not that he comes in for particular criticism; it seems rather as if the stature he has gained since the outbreak of the war was taken for granted: after all, the society as a whole is surpassing itself. Not even Zelenskyy's Russian-Jewish ethnicity seems to interest anyone, positively or negatively.

I'm not going to give you the information you want to hear, the psychiatrist Semen Gluzman told me time after time when I asked him in Kyiv about Zelenskyy's Jewishness. Naturally he was aware why the question comes up for a visitor from Germany. Gluzman is a Jew himself; he spent seven years in a work camp as a dissident in the Soviet Union, then three years banished to Siberia, and he has spoken out against every government so far in Ukraine. Yes, he voted for Zelenskyy, he concedes, but only to vote his predecessor out, and he regretted it when he saw the people the new president surrounds himself with; no, he will certainly not vote for him again.

But isn't there some importance, seventy-seven years after the Shoah, to the fact that the country fighting for Europe as no other today is led by a Jew?

I'm not going to give you the information you want to hear, Gluzman repeats.

Perhaps this is the information in a European country: that the president's religion is of no importance.

Near Chernihiv we come to a road in which the Ukrainian and the Russian forces stood face to face. The front line was marked by an earthwork that was passable only on foot. But although the road is clear again, how far the Russians advanced will be visible for a long time yet, because the houses are intact from that point on. Who had the worst of it? On this side of the line, the inhabitants were rained on by shells; on the other side, they were ruled by the occupiers. I asked around, but no one wanted to decide whether peace or freedom is more important – putting it dramatically myself. In front of a municipal building I saw a flowerbed with something sprouting in it. I assumed it would be potatoes or something of the sort, because the fields lay fallow on account of the mines, and no shops would open for a long time yet. No, those are flowers, said a woman standing next to me.

In Chernihiv itself we were surprised to see that the city centre has remained largely intact and even looks well kept. I had heard many times that 70 per cent of the city had been destroyed: that was what people in Kyiv and Lviv had told me. In fact, only a few buildings have been damaged: here a hotel, there a government agency. When I mentioned that, the philosopher Anton Drobovich in Kyiv said that the country wasn't doing itself any favours by exaggerating the damage, although it was probably inevitable in the rumour amplifier of social media. The real destruction is disastrous enough, he said. Drobovich is the head of Ukraine's Institute of National Remembrance, and he met with me not in his office but on a park bench near his barracks. He too had volunteered and was wearing a simple soldier's uniform, which looked a bit curious, since his words, glances and gestures were still those of the taciturn, cautiously deliberating man of books. At the moment, they were digging trenches all around Kyiv in case the Russians should advance on the capital again.

Genocide, for example, Drobovich continued, is a clearly defined legal term which should not be used hastily, otherwise it will be devalued. There are many war crimes that are now sufficiently documented, but whether Russia is actually committing genocide against the Ukrainians – that would require evidence that would have to be verified by an independent body, and it would need diligence and time; otherwise we would be imitating Putin, who tosses the term around indiscriminately. No matter how great their suffering and how understandable their anger – that is precisely what the Ukrainians are fighting for: the rule of law, not capriciousness. So they would have to be precise especially in that accusation.

While I ride the night train towards the West, there are increasing indications and predictions that a major Russian offensive is impending. Will the enemy troops be repulsed, or will they entrench themselves throughout the Donbas, along the Black Sea coast, perhaps as far as Moldova? That is what the further course of the conflict depends on, the analyses say. One way or the other, many signs point to a protracted positional war that would divide one part of the country from the other. Will the cohesion, the high degree of mobilization, the impressive solidarity then continue? Human beings have such a great longing for normality.

On my arrival in Lviv, with the usual couple of hours' delay, I am amazed at how life has returned to this gorgeous city. The pedestrian zone, where many shops were still closed a few days ago, is now full of people, and the buskers and the musicians and jugglers are once again competing for their attention and money. The weather, finally a bit warmer, and a few rays of sunshine top it off to make the war a bit more remote.

In a café I meet Olga Pikula, thirty-nine years old, from Mariupol. Now I'm not at all the mountain-climber type or anything like that, she explains, and she is perfectly credible with her elegant outfit – and her delicate stature. During the siege, she learned how to gather wood and cook on an open fire; she learned to chop ice to melt it for water; she learned to find something edible in the garden and to warm her blankets so that she wouldn't freeze in her sleep at 8 degrees below zero. She learned to overcome her fear of the constant shelling when she fetched water, sprinting from one doorway to the next. She learned to persevere as she carried the two 6-litre canisters the 3 kilometres back home: her biceps still show it. She learned to surprise herself when she persuaded her husband to get in the car and flee, immediately, during a brief ceasefire on 15 March. On the road, a shot hit the car directly in front of them, with a child in the back seat.

Olga is a businesswoman; she owned several private educational centres in Mariupol; she was involved in the municipal assembly; she speaks fluent English and is well travelled. She wanted to go skiing with friends in the Carpathians, then put the holiday back a week, and suddenly the war started. For three weeks she was living on another planet.

I learned another thing, she says: I have learned to hate. I didn't even know what it meant before. That is the most terrible thing: that I know now what hate is. I hate Russia; everyone who has been through that hates Russia.

And have you learned anything else?

Yes, I have learned how the people must have felt in Aleppo in 2015. To be honest, that didn't interest me at all at the time. I have learned how people in Africa feel who are starving, who are afraid, who don't know whether they will see another sunrise. I feel with them now, physically. I think that was the most important lesson.

When I ask whether she can imagine returning to Mariupol, Olga answers with a question: What Mariupol? Then she takes out her smartphone and shows me a video that was evidently taken using a drone. It is hard to imagine how one could exaggerate the destruction that is visible in the pictures. No, for the time being, she will stay in Lviv, or move to Kyiv; she doesn't know yet, says Olga. In any case, she wants to start up her language and professional development courses again, online now, and is hoping for a loan. For the future, though, she has a very definite dream. She once visited Strasbourg before the war, and she wants to return there one day to work at the World Forum for Democracy, under the auspices of the Council of Europe, the pan-European human rights organization.

Reconciliation with enemies is one part of belonging to Europe. People like Olga Pikula, who feel, physically, with the most wretched, but have also learned what hate is, could one day be our teachers.

32

The Dust on All the Faces

In South Madagascar, Farming Families Battle to Survive a Lethal Drought Caused by Climate Change

Die Zeit, 22 September 2022

There is the dust on all the faces because there is not enough water even to slake the people's thirst. Cooking, too, is more important than washing: cassava or rice with boiled sweet-potato leaves; the sweet potatoes themselves are all gone. There are the red lips, as if from lipstick, where cactus fruits have become the staple. Yes, there are the children's distended bellies and the men's thin legs. Where there are still livestock, there are the ox carts hauling mounds of yellow canisters from village to village, each canister holding 20 litres of water. There are the prices of the canisters, which cost more the farther the water has been hauled. But where the way to water is particularly long, most of the oxen are already sold or dead. Then you see whole columns of thin, bowed figures, carrying poles on their necks with a canister at each end. From the source to the consumer we have logged 5, 7, even 15 kilometres on the odometer of our pickup. Where do you get the strength? we ask one of them. He sets his 40 kilos on the ground and answers: he has a wife and children. From love, then, I think, and I know that

that is much too romantic. Where then? It must be more elementary than love.

Are you angry with him? I ask a woman whose husband said he was going to look for work elsewhere because the soil didn't yield crops any more. He never got in touch again. Now she lives with three children in a refugee camp near the market in the city of Ambovombe. 'Camp' sounds as if there is something. In fact there is the parking lot for the ox carts, around which seventy households have pitched their tents. Tents? Nothing but a couple of poles draped at waist height with plastic sheeting from used rice sacks. When there is no market, the children play football on the square. Many of the children are sick, though: coughs, headaches, diarrhoea, or rashes. No wonder, living on a paddock.

No, I am not angry with him, the woman answers; if he loved me, I would show him my anger, but as it is I don't waste any time on him. Collecting wood every day with the children, selling it at the market and buying my mother something to eat – she is too old to go with us to the woods – I don't have the strength to be angry. Her income: 1,000 to 3,000 ariary a day, the equivalent of 25 to 75 cents. That is enough for a little bit of noodles or a little bit of rice with practically nothing else. At least there is a water tap here, just one for seventy households and the livestock, and the owner of the lot is a generous man. Sometimes he gives the refugees some food or brings medicine for the children. Twice a year some organization brings a few sacks of rice. Most of the aid organizations that hurried to southern Madagascar in autumn 2021, after the United Nations declared the world's first climate-caused famine, have since cut back their work or moved it to the eastern coast, where a series of cyclones came through in February 2022. And the drought threatens to cause famines throughout eastern Africa this autumn, while the available aid money has not increased – although every sack of rice and every ladle of beans has risen in price by a quarter since the outbreak of the European war, which is as far off to the people here as the wars in Yemen or in Ethiopia are to Westerners. And, before Russia's attack on Ukraine, the pandemic had already plunged the economy into a severe crisis, while no one had reserves to draw on, not the state and certainly not the people of one of the poorest countries in the world. And in front of the next tent, immobile, sits a frail older man who also tells us his story:

He took out a loan to buy seed, then the crop failed, and so he had to sell his livestock. When the crops failed for the fifth time in a row, he sold his land too and sought his fortune in the city; that was two years ago. Since then, two more harvests have failed in southern Madagascar, normally a fertile country. His wife died before they reached the camp; he misses her very much, he says. The two children who still live with him collect wood in the forest. He himself worked carrying water, but now he is too weak for it. On market days he begs and gets a few ariary or some food. When all the children have gone, if not before, he will stop begging. Then he'll just stay sitting in front of his tent.

There are the forests that are disappearing; there are the many tree stumps along the wayside, vast areas where there is nothing but stumps left standing. Besides the water canisters, what you see most along the tracks and in the markets are the charcoal sacks. What else are you going to use to cook your rice if there is no electricity grid even in the towns, no gas, no running water, no asphalt as far as the eye can see? At a little stand with charcoal sacks we stop. To the right of the track is a nature reserve, which makes us realize what it must have looked like to the left of the track just a few years ago: green with the leaves and the plants spreading between the tree trunks. Now we see to the left a wood that consists more of brown gaps than of trees. A tiny hut with a window-sized hatch through which business is transacted, a back room, and in this tiny building live more than twenty people, we learn to our amazement. Now they all look at us expectantly, from the door, from the window, from in front of the hut, evidently just as amazed as we are. For nine years they've been selling charcoal, and by now that is their sole source of income, because they have harvested practically nothing in the past seven years. How much does a sack cost? The equivalent of $1.90, although actually they haven't sold any in the last month because the charcoal is cheaper further east, where there is still more forest. Next month, they hope, the price will go up again there; all it needs is for something to happen. What's supposed to happen? I ask. After the cyclones in February, they were able to charge over $3 a sack; those won't have been the last cyclones. And what happens when all their land is deforested? I won't cut down more than half, says the father, so something will be left for the children. And when your children have cut down the other half, what then? Then I won't be around any more. Have you never thought about cutting only as many trees as you can replant? No, we haven't got the money for saplings. When we sell a sack, we spend all the money on rice.

I wonder that the nature reserve across the road still seems to be untouched. And their own woods, aren't they also threatened? How do they protect them from wood thieves, who must exist, considering the poverty? No, not here, says the father; to us the woods are sacred; we have learned that from our ancestors. People who cut down someone else's trees will have bad luck. So they cut down only their own future.

There is our shame. Have you any idea why it doesn't rain? I ask. No, that must be God's will, the charcoal-seller answers; neither he nor anyone else among the thirsty people has ever heard the term 'climate change'. And I stand before them, from one of the countries that produce the most greenhouse-gas emissions, while Madagascar's contribution is just 0.01 per cent. They know even less about colonialism, which marked the beginning of the exploitation of nature in Madagascar, as elsewhere. The war in Ukraine, which has made so many foods prohibitively expensive, is also unknown to them. It is almost a consolation that Covid too is very far away. That word they have heard, and they say: at least that disease is only found in the cities. The fact that tourism has collapsed, and with it the state's revenues – that is not noticeable either in southern Madagascar. Even before the pandemic, the state invested hardly anything in the south, not in the past thirty, forty years. There is an elite that has taken over the colonial rulers' looting. Actually Madagascar would be a rich country: it has vanilla, minerals, gold, sapphires; it has fantastic national parks, endless beaches, some of the greatest biodiversity in the world. As recently as the late 1960s the people were full of hope; the educational system, the infrastructure, the gross domestic product, the arts were developing quite well for postcolonial conditions, but that was before most of the mineral resources had been discovered.

There are the bridges that have become redundant because the river has run dry or is just a trickle in which the people bathe, wash clothes, water the livestock, wash a truck, refill the yellow canisters. When you look at the scene from above, the wide, dry riverbed of brownish-yellow sand looks like a painting by Hieronymus Bosch, composed of countless little vignettes. Not all of them are scenes of hell; it is beautiful to see the children splashing in the water. And how dignified the people are as they wash themselves, men and women, when there is no privacy to be had; their genitals always covered with one hand, their backs always turned to one another.

There are the fields that have been planted: sweet potatoes, beans, scallions, cassava. The cyclones that devastated the east coast seemed a blessing to the south because they finally brought rain, a lot of rain. Those who could still afford seed planted their fields. And, yes, in many fields you can see that something is growing, if meagrely. If it doesn't rain before autumn, it will all die again. There are parents who remember how, when they were children, they ate their fill every day.

We talk with a family that has more land than others. How much exactly? The father stretches out his arm and moves it from left to right. None of it inherited. Their vigour, their perspicacity, their love for their profession, too, shine in his and in his wife's eyes, which even at their advanced age have a graceful beauty. The family's hut is made of corrugated steel, not of wood like the others, and is painted red and green. The children go to school; three of them have already finished high school. I may be mistaken, but I think I see their prosperity not only in the orderliness in the hut, the plastic chairs, the clean dishes on the shelves, the suitcases stacked carefully against the walls. No, I think I also see that they are better off by the couple's tender looks and loving touches. Among the very poor I have not observed any tenderness between adults. But now this family's livelihood too is crumbling, or is already half destroyed. The next source of water is 20 kilometres away; a canister costs 2,000 ariary; it is brought by ox cart. They need two of them every day, and then they still haven't bought any food. How are they supposed to pay for it all, and the school fees besides, and the upkeep for the children at university? In their region, not quite at the epicentre of the drought, the last harvest was four years ago now. They have been drawing on their savings for a long time already, and working their big fields all by themselves. They could give up their land and move to the city; they still have the means to do so without ending up in a tent camp; they have relatives there who would take them in until they have made a new start. Why are they still here? It is the land of our ancestors, is the answer, as I expected.

The ancestors, one quickly learns in Madagascar, the ancestors are not dead; they are as present as this table, this neighbour, this tree. And, with the ancestors, the afterlife. The only concrete buildings we see along the track are tombs, and sometimes we discover a whole village living in the middle of the fields for a couple of weeks to build one of these complexes together. The only feasts we encounter are funerals, but only when someone has died in old age – that is, at fifty, sixty years. Then, yes, then the people dance, drink and laugh. I believe that offers a great deal of reassurance with which to bear the conditions of the present: when it is only the lesser part of reality anyway. So far, the people who flee their villages are comparatively few, and when we asked those on the ox-cart parking lot, all of them talked about going back to be with their ancestors as soon as the sky sends rain again. At most, individual family members go away to earn some money that they can share with those who stay where the ancestors are.

We reach the heart of darkness some 200 kilometres, or a day's journey with the four-wheel-drive pickup, from Ambovombe, which has a little airport for United Nations aid flights. That is no doubt why all the aid organizations are concentrated there, and, when politicians come, they visit the nearby villages; what they see there is shocking enough. A day later, west of the town of Ampanihy to be exact, we see hardly any of the white jeeps. There are children who no longer play, children who have lost even their imaginations, children who are not curious about the strangers. There is a teacher who asks his pupils to write something on the chalkboard, because we are surprised to hear that they can read and write, one sentence at least. A girl, seven, eight years old, stands up and slowly writes: *Kememoho*. I realize that it means something terrible by the shocked looks of the others before they translate the sentence for me: 'I am hungry.'

There are villages, whole villages, that come to meet us as soon as we open the doors of the pickup. At first I think the inhabitants are begging for food or money when they surround us, but I soon realize that they aren't familiar with people distributing aid, or at least they aren't expecting it. We sit in a circle in the middle of the village and listen. They are also unaccustomed, I gradually become aware, to talking about their situation, giving voice to their hearts. But there comes a point, and it would probably come anywhere in the world, at which they speak out spontaneously: when I ask who has lost a child to starvation. In one village, three speak up; in another, fifteen; or they answer that it will happen this autumn at the latest if the rain doesn't come. I look at the children's dull eyes, their swollen bellies, the snot on their upper lips because their noses are running constantly, and I don't have to be a doctor to know that the fear is all too justified. One of these children who are now staring at me motionlessly will die then, or two or three or still more.

There is the story that, strangely, always sounds similar when a child starves to death, and it is quite different from how I had imagined it: the child is not lying down, but sitting upright on the ground, their hands around their knees. Then suddenly the potbelly drops, really, so that from the side you can see it fall, and then the child falls over all at once. If it is daytime, the parents are usually in the bush looking for food, which here consists mostly just of cactus leaves and cactus fruits. Someone is sent to fetch them, but doesn't tell them right away that their child is dead. The shock, we are told every time, the shock would be too great. Something has happened, they call to the parents from a distance, come quickly. But I knew right away what had happened, says one of the fathers, who ran back to the village.

Some places, there is music, which is glad tidings. With the drought, the culture dies out too; there was nothing besides agriculture and feasts before, and, without the one, no one has money for the other. Southern Madagascar is famous for its musicians, but we ask about them in vain. And so it transfixes us like a choir of angels when, on the drive to the coast, we discover a big, yes, almost a huge crowd on a village square, and through the open windows a tinny electric guitar, like a sound out of a Detroit garage, and a breathless beat blow in. Funeral! cries one of my companions, and the other adds, If there is music, you know that we're back up to the minimum subsistence level.

We get out and make our way through to a pickup truck with two huge loudspeakers mounted above its covered bed. On the bed of the truck are a drummer, a singer, and an ultra-cool man playing security guard. Next to the truck is a diesel generator, its noise being drowned out by the music. But where is the electric guitar coming from? We go around the truck and find the young rhythm guitarist sitting next to the driver, and alone in the back seat the aged band leader, playing wild solos while nevertheless nodding at us as nonchalantly as Keith Richards. Red baseball cap, dark sunglasses, Hawaiian shirt and moustache trimmed thin. The crowd – men, women, old people, children – dance ecstatically, some even spilling their expensive beer. It is the proximity to the sea, we learn, that provides the village with food, a little income and, because of the income, music.

There is the realization of how little human beings really need: only soil, a wood, a lake, a river or a sea that offers them enough food; after that the superfluous begins, the impractical, the beautiful, making their lives rich. There is the water that the children spray at each other because there is enough of it. There is the perplexity because humanity has more than an abundance of all goods but distributes them so inadequately. Madagascar itself has enough of everything, but it also has a government that spends 95 per cent of its revenue in the capital because it has perpetuated the centralization of the colonial rulers and survives only thanks to Western aid. There would have to be roads, electricity, wells, water pipelines to distribute the goods that there are, if the rain won't fall. Instead the world community, meaning only the rich countries of course, distributes some money and a few sacks of rice to avoid having to see pictures of starvation and death. And, where nothing is distributed, no one is looking anyway. Nonetheless, the question remains, nowhere as dramatically as in southern Madagascar perhaps, why the modern age, of all eras, doesn't seem to have heard of the future.

On the beach of the tiny coastal town of Beheloka, we meet the fisherman Christophe Germain Mananandroko, sitting between two canoes. Strong build, balding with white hair cut short, a white jersey with the sleeves cut off and the French football association's FFF logo, Fédération française de football, which coincidentally is the abbreviation of the climate-action organization Fridays for Future. And in fact Christophe, who has some schooling and an old, small smartphone, has heard quite a bit about climate change and knows that the drought very probably has to do with it. But – only the drought? About the same time as the drought began, the wind became much stronger, so that Christophe can only go out fishing twice a week on average, and when he notices that the wind is coming up he rows back to shore straight away. But many of his younger colleagues are first-generation fishermen and don't know the warning signs. Just three months ago, on the same night, two of them didn't come home from the sea. But the sea, the sea – even if the wind doesn't blow, it's no longer the sea he knows. Christophe remembers perfectly: when he was young, ten, fifteen years old, he only had to stand knee-deep in the water and hundreds, thousands of fish flurried around his legs. Catching 5 kilos took no time at all. Now you go out in the water, Christophe says, and you don't see any fish at all, not one. Even beyond the reef there aren't many left. The night before last he was out with his son, bright moon and calm sea, put out at eight, back at four, and what did they catch? One and a half kilos, barely enough for lunch for the big family. It used to be that he could put something aside, buy the children a few presents: not any more; the grandchildren don't get any.

Is it because of the industrial fishing? I ask. Yes, there are big Japanese ships out there; they have a treaty with the state. But they've been around a long time; the industrial ships can't be the only reason. So maybe the depletion of the fish is connected with the wind? And the wind with climate change? I don't know, Christophe answers, but our main problem is a different one anyway. What is it? Our main problem is that the coral reef is almost completely destroyed now, and we did that ourselves. The reef is the fishes' home; they all throng there; every fisherman knows that. We have one of the longest coral reefs in the Indian Ocean, and now there is hardly anything to be caught there; we have to go farther and farther out to sea to catch anything at all, but out there there's the problem of the waves; our boats aren't made for that.

Is there no one who explains the connections to the fishermen?

There are programmes to raise the fishermen's awareness, by the World Wildlife Fund (WWF), by Blue Ventures, by the Madagascar national parks organization, but they only explain what the fishermen already know, Christophe says: that's nothing new; the fishermen already know their lives depend on the reef.

Then why are they destroying it? I ask. Why are they destroying their own future?

There is a new generation, Christophe answers; there are more and more people living in the villages, and more and more of them go to sea because their land doesn't yield crops any more. They come from the whole inland region now to catch fish, but they don't know how it's done. Cast their nets over the reef; fix them to the reef; anchor on the reef; they even walk on the reef; no one used to do any of that before.

Before when?

When I was young, let's say forty years ago, no fisherman ever so much as touched the reef. We didn't need any WWF; our ancestors forbade us.

And why have the people lost their relationship to the sea?

Greed, Christophe answers straight away, it is greed. Then he tells us of one of the fishermen in the village who has bought special nets to catch more fish, which in turn gets him more money. Of the little that is still there, this man, a neighbour, catches everything and doesn't even leave the others what's left. This greed for more and more, we never knew that before, no one among us; we were all more or less equal.

How do you see the future of fishing?

Bad, very bad; it will disappear here completely, I'm afraid.

Don't the programmes have any effect at all?

Nonsense. At the training the people say, 'Yes, yes,' and the next day they carry on as they have been.

Then the cause is in the people themselves?

Yes, we're to blame, we ourselves; we know it and do it anyway. The cause is: the people's minds are sinking lower.

But the people can't help climate change, they can't help that it doesn't rain; that the wind has grown so strong.

Yes, I know, they can't help that.

What do you think, then, why is it, I ask, human beings are so clever, just take this smartphone here – mine – there's so much intelligence in it, in such a tiny device, so much inventiveness, cunning, technical skill. So why are human beings destroying the Earth, although their lives depend on it?

Christophe laughs sadly and says nothing.

Have you really no idea? I insist. I don't know, myself; I've come all this way, from far Germany to here, and I haven't found any answer.

Christophe takes my smartphone from my hand – it is newer and bigger than his – and he says, look, this device, this has a huge memory. Thirty gigabytes, a hundred gigabytes, two hundred gigabytes?

I am surprised that an old fisherman in a tiny, remote village on the south coast of Madagascar, several days' journey from the nearest asphalt road – that this man knows the word 'gigabyte'. And at the same time I am not surprised, after having heard sharp guitar riffs and racing beats in a still more remote village.

In this smartphone alone, Christophe continues, there is so much more memory than any human being has. But this memory is nothing compared to the memory of nature. The memory of nature goes back much further; it goes back to the beginning of the world's creation.

There is also the fisherman Christophe Germain Mananandroko, who seems to know more than we do.

33

WOMAN, LIFE, FREEDOM
The Uprising in Iran, July–December 2022

Die Zeit, 14 July 2022

Years ago in a cinema in Cologne I saw a film about a special unit of the Iranian secret police. It told of the murders of writers and intellectuals, enhanced interrogation techniques and coerced confessions; of cowardice and heroism in a society in which a person can save his own life by betraying his colleagues. Scenes such as the one in which the commander of the unit watches a TV show and fixes himself a snack while he is waiting for a dissident to die of the poison he has been injected with – it was high drama, as suspenseful as anything Hollywood can offer. But it was not a drama.

From the scraps of conversation that I heard on my way out of the cinema and on the pavement outside, I noticed that the other spectators thought they had seen a gripping espionage thriller. Those who remembered the Iran of the 1990s, at the time of the serial murders of writers, knew that nothing in the film was fictional and nothing exaggerated; some characters had been altered, but not enough to make their real-life models unrecognizable. It was Iran's political and literary reality in life size: if not in the documentary sense, then in the faces, the gestures, the events, the beliefs – down to the prayers that the agents recited when they executed their victims. I couldn't believe that a film portrayed so minutely that darkest of the many dark times of Iranian literature, and that it had not been shot abroad, but secretly in Tehran. Naturally there were no credits, except for the name of the director.

Since then, since his spectacular film exposé *Manuscripts Don't Burn*, it was clear that Mohammad Rasoulof was in danger not only of being arrested but of losing his life. He was undeterred by his repeated arrests, his six-year prison sentence, the threats he can hardly count any more; he was also uninterested in the offers from foreign countries and continued to film in Iran. In 2020 he smuggled *There Is No Evil* out of the country and won the Golden Bear – the jury, critics and audiences at the Berlin Film Festival unanimous for once. By showing the troubled conscience, the excuses and the day-to-day cares of ordinary Iranian executioners, the film both identifies the society's present condition and transcends it in a drama of Cain and Abel. I was not only appalled at Iran; I was appalled at human beings as Rasoulof brought forth the little, sad truth behind their façade, which is also my truth. Weeks later I was still going through my day as if stunned.

But the truth of human beings also includes their ability to surpass themselves. Since last Friday, Mohammad Rasoulof has been in solitary confinement, one of the most important filmmakers of our time. The same day, his colleague Mostafa al-Ahmad was arrested; at the moment, the Iranian prisons are full of political prisoners again, apparently without anyone being troubled by it in the West, where the hope is to save the nuclear treaty. Now the solidarity of the entire film world is needed – associations, academies and festivals – and also the protest of the German government and the European Commission, so that Rasoulof's art, his incredible courage, his depth may go on singing in our hearts.

PS: I had barely sent this text to the editors when, in the same hour, I received the news that Jafar Panahi has also been arrested. He has been arrested before, when he was sentenced to six years in prison and prohibited from making films for twenty years, and in 2015 he was the first to win the Golden Bear in Berlin with a film shot in secret. Now Panahi has spoken out, together with many other filmmakers, in support of Rasoulof and al-Ahmad. In the days to come there will certainly be more arrests, until finally no one is left in the most magnificent and desperate filmmaking country in the world. I ought to write a new article, in fact one for every single person who is being persecuted in Iran for their art, their faith, their beliefs. Forgive me; today I can no more.

Die Zeit, 6 October 2022

The course the protests in Iran will take is probably this: the state will attack the demonstrators, as it has already begun to do, with firearms, arrests, torture, executions. In the funereal calm that follows, another wave of emigration will begin. Not long afterwards there will be a new occasion for those who remain to take to the streets again; all they will have to do is shake off their fatigue, their fear, their pain. The West will applaud their courage and their will to freedom for a few days. And will soon want to do business with the Islamic Republic again.

That is the course events will probably take. And yet some things are different about the current protests compared with 2009, 2017 or 2019, when thousands or even millions of people joined the demonstrations. The rebellion has a definite theme – equality – a burning topic in the day-to-day lives of half of the population, and everywhere the men are finally declaring solidarity with the women. Equally new is the fact that the call for freedom, the rule of law and emancipation, which is mainly a middle-class demand, is linked with the critical distress of the poorer population. Up to now, these two classes have mostly demonstrated separately for their partially different interests. Another new factor is that the protests are not confined to particular centres or regions: they still go on without leadership, or even offices; the flow of information is also severely impeded by the government's restrictions on the internet. But the institutional weakness is also a potential advantage, because the movement cannot be crushed by arresting its leaders and by isolated, highly visible massacres. The unrest has already been going on longer than any previous protest since the founding of the Islamic Republic in 1979.

But another factor, also new and especially dangerous to the regime, is the ethnic aspect: the woman killed, Mahsa Amini, was a Kurd. Forty-five per cent of Iranians speak Persian as their mother tongue. In Kurdistan, Baluchistan and Azerbaijan, the regime cannot organize assemblies to create the appearance of democracy, not even by means of buses, meals and holiday coupons; in those regions, militias from other parts of the country have to be deployed to suppress the protests – personnel that is then lacking in Tehran, Mashhad or Isfahan. After having completely neutralized that part of the elite which is amenable to reform, and having put those politicians in prison or under house arrest who just yesterday were members of the Majlis, government ministers or even president, the regime is running out of people who could at least manage the country, to say nothing of bringing peace and security.

But, sadly, there is another new thing about the current rebellion: the German government's hesitation to criticize the Islamic Republic. For months now, the already bleak human rights situation has been deteriorating dramatically. Executions are being carried out in public again, and up to July their numbers have already more than doubled over the previous year to 251. Among many other critics of the regime, two of Iran's most famous filmmakers have been arrested, Mohammad Rasoulof and Jafar Panahi, both winners of the Berlin film festival's Golden Bear; the persecution of the Baha'i religious minority is intensifying, and a few weeks ago a revolutionary court sentenced the two LGBT activists Zahra Sedighi-Hamadani and Elham Choobdar to death. The reactions of the German government, the European Union? Below the threshold of perception. Even when Iranians all over the country were protesting against oppression, nothing was heard from the Green foreign minister Annalena Baerbock for days before she finally brought herself to make a terse statement in New York about women's rights. It would have been good to hear just a tenth of the pathos with which she generally praises the likewise heroic struggle of the Ukrainian people. Increasingly criticized for her passivity, Baerbock now pleads for sanctions and carefully avoids mentioning details. Chancellor Olaf Scholz also expresses only a few platitudes, through his government spokesman. If we remember – and many Iranians do so, not only in Germany – the empathy with which Angela Merkel addressed the Iranian demonstrators in 2009, for example, setting them in relation to her own East German biography and the fall of the Berlin Wall, her successor's tight-lipped response cannot be explained by his northern-German temperament alone.

Is it due to concern that a civil war could ensue if the regime falls? That much strategic calculation would be surprising in German foreign policy, which has excelled time and again in recent years by its short-sightedness: witness Russia, witness Afghanistan, witness the present Green foreign minister's refusal to reform Europe's institutions. No, the reason is probably much more trivial: is the German government concerned about the nuclear negotiations with Tehran, whose success would bring access to Iran's gigantic natural gas reserves? That would be another disastrous mistake of Germany's realpolitik – or, rather, its energy policy. Because there is no reliable nuclear treaty to be made with this regime, which no longer has any footing except armed force: it is rotten to the core; its ideology is no more than a framework of lies; the economy in Iran has hit bottom, the environmental destruction is tremendous, and the only thing that is more frightening is the lack of any vision for the future; the post-fossil era, which will dawn rather sooner than later in Iran too, is something the regime is not even thinking about because it no longer expects to be in power that long.

History is made of developments that were once improbable. Perhaps history will be made in the coming days in Iran, or at the next uprising, or the one after that. For the German government to allow doubts to arise as to which side it is on is thus not only a moral failing. It is also disastrous with regard to Germany's own national interest.

Die Zeit, 19 October 2022

Reaching for the phone on waking to see the night's videos: thus another day starts for millions of Iranians around the world. The very fact that the uprising is now entering its fifth week goes against all predictions, mine included. Monday morning, the images of the Evin Prison fire in the north of Tehran, the flames visible from afar, the billowing smoke almost palpable, the salvos of gunshots audible in the city of nine million inhabitants. What news of Jafar Panahi, what of Mohammad Rasoulof, the two filmmakers? It is both unjust and human to worry first about the prisoners you know. Four deaths are reported, later eight, but no names.

Some of the jittery videos show great numbers of relatives waiting outside the burning prison for news, protesting with increasing anger; the traffic jam on the nearby motorways; horns honking in protest and women standing on the roofs of the cars shouting 'Death to the dictator', over and over again, 'Death to the dictator'. The dictator will know that that slogan is meant more literally with every demonstrator shot, and especially with every child killed – they are said to number twenty-three so far. So the soldiers have to shoot still more protesters: it is now a life-and-death struggle between the ruler and the people. But the people are eighty million strong.

The regime's own violence forces it to use ever more violence, the exit of evolutionary change was passed up years ago, and now repression no longer works as it used to do. Prominent faces of loyal public figures show their horror at the brutality: sports stars, television announcers and even the regime's court poet, Reza Amirkhani. Probably not even a massacre such as that of 2019, with over 1,500 demonstrators shot, would be enough any more to suppress the rebellion. Instead of mass protests in Tehran, which have become too dangerous, demonstrators gather for smaller, often clandestine actions, which cannot be thwarted everywhere at once, and which generate new videos daily.

A friend of Rasoulof's answers me with a voice message that he still hasn't heard any news of Rasoulof, but Panahi was allowed to call his wife in the early hours; she says he is safe now, but it was the worst night of his life. The prisoners fleeing the burning buildings were greeted in the courtyard with tear gas. That is yet another unconfirmed account which, like the hagiographies of old, is passed along through a chain of several informants. And, at the moment, there seem to be more heroes in Iran than anywhere else in the world.

Another video shows the writer Amir Hassan Cheheltan speaking to the German television network ZDF from his home in Tehran, walls of books in the background. The flat is only a stone's throw from Evin Prison; I have visited him there often. This is a revolution now, says Cheheltan: from his mouth the word is particularly weighty, as he is one of the more cautious people – and because he is saying it in Tehran to a foreign broadcaster. Although – or because – he is just a stone's throw from Evin Prison. Are you in Tehran?! I text him immediately – because I cannot believe he dared return to Iran after his reading tour of Europe, during which he wrote acerbic articles and gave critical interviews – Are you in safety? He sends another voice message to say he's all right so far; he had no trouble entering the country. It is difficult to talk; the internet is too slow for live connections, but one-way voice messages go through.

The longing of Iranians living abroad to get on a plane has probably never been as great as it is in these days. Dual citizens especially risk being paraded on television as foreign agitators and held as hostages to be exchanged for Iranian secret agents. But being in Germany, where hardly anyone seems to be concerned about Iran, feels more wrong than ever. Even in the cultural scene, where battle is resolutely joined for gender equality and against all forms of discrimination, hardly anything is heard on the protests in Iran: no theatre changes its programme; only authors with Iranian backgrounds decry the German government's Iran policy; no cinema commemorates the Berlinale winners arrested in Iran.

Sports? Women cannot enter football stadiums, women athletes are handicapped in international competition by their obligatory clothing, and football pros are in Evin Prison for their tweets criticizing the government. But not even in Dortmund has the murder of the sixteen-year-old demonstrator Sarina Esmailzadeh, who was a true fan of Borussia Dortmund, been grounds for a minute of mourning. Only a few spirited fans unfurled a poster to commemorate her.

And the politicians? Annalena Baerbock is frenetically cheered at the Green Party convention, although her long silence on the protests is a complete sell-out of her vaunted feminist foreign policy. The European sanctions that she now suddenly claims to have initiated are harmless, as if they were intended more to relieve the pressure on her personally than to exert pressure on the dictatorship in Iran. Omid Nouripur, the member of the Bundestag who was born in Iran, provides entertainment as a hopping, roistering DJ while in Evin the political prisoners are in danger of burning to death in their cells: this too a video that will remain part of the record. *Bi-sharaf*, my nearly ninety-year-old mother called the Green Party co-chairman: 'dishonourable' – and although it sounds harmless in English, in Persian it is one of the worst possible imprecations. Once upon a time the Greens, if any party at all, could be depended on when it came to defending human rights. Now there is nobody home, and I do not mean that in a figurative sense.

Recently, when several thousand students were surrounded at Sharif University, they broadcast their discussion live to the world on Twitter. Apparently they knew who is on which side of history, because they complained more than once about the lack of solidarity from Berlin in particular. Germany has evidently learned nothing from its misguided Russia policy, which was all about energy and stability and now leaves us with neither one. Now at least the pictures are coming in of drones that Iran allegedly supplied to Russia. If that is confirmed, Europe could yet adopt sanctions that strike the regime. The demonstrators being killed day after day in Iran are apparently not sufficient grounds. Caring for Europeans first is unjust, but human, my German compatriots might reply. One of the most impressive videos of recent days shows hundreds of schoolgirls, fourteen, fifteen years old, shouting down an officer trying to speak to them from a podium. So much energy in the high voices – I would have been afraid too if I had been at the podium, so much more afraid than I would have been of alleged or actual rioters. You have no future here, the girls tell him. Most recently, it is mainly images from the provinces that find their way out of the country, such as those from Zahedan in eastern Iran, where thousands took to the streets after Friday prayers. After Friday prayers, note: the simple people, to judge by their clothes and beards. Two weeks ago, the security forces there caused a bloodbath after Friday prayers, killing at least sixty-six demonstrators.

In other videos of the weekend, security forces are seen shooting at demonstrators with machine guns posted on the roofs, as in Sanandaj, the capital of Iranian Kurdistan. Iran's most prominent female climber, Elnaz Rekabi, winner of the bronze medal at last year's world championships, has stirred people's hearts. On Sunday at the Asian championships in Seoul, she took off her headscarf before scaling the wall wearing the national colours. All of this, one video after another, on the smartphone screen on getting up in the morning.

Finally, the message arrives that Rasoulof too has survived the night. Another day begins which the millions of Iranians living abroad will go through as foreigners because their thoughts are with their compatriots. And in Iran, more videos are being made, so that the rest of the world too may finally look.

The day ends with pictures from Iranian state television showing the gratitude of prisoners in Evin Prison, and with

Annalena Baerbock on the news being asked no critical questions about her Iran policy: state television here too. The next morning, Tuesday, begins with the news that Elnaz Rekabi has disappeared in Seoul and is said to have been abducted to Iran. If that is confirmed, then in the days to come she can be expected to perform the remorse to which she will have been coerced under torture. Like so many Iranian women before her who dared to stand up for their rights. That will not disturb any of Germany's political parties as long as their quota of women candidates is fufilled.

Die Zeit, 3 November 2022

The speech by the president of Germany, Frank-Walter Steinmeier, on Friday in Bellevue Palace marks the failure of a German realpolitik which fostered exactly what it was intended to prevent: a large-scale war in Europe and high energy costs. And at the same time, with the metaphysically charged term 'evil' which the president attributed to Putin's Russia, the speech stands for the danger that Germany's misconceived pragmatism will backfire, turning into a Manichaean struggle that can only end in annihilation or submission.

But while Berlin claims to have learned a lesson from its realpolitik in dealing with Russia, it continues to practise realpolitik at its finest towards another authoritarian regime. Much has already been written about the foreign minister's initial silence. The sanctions that the EU has finally adopted are merely symbolic. Yes, after the use of Iranian drones in Ukraine, Baerbock promised that there would be no 'business as usual' in Iran policy. And on Monday, after seven long weeks, Chancellor Scholz finally condemned the violence of the Iranian security forces in a tweet. But no member of the

German government dares approach the grail of German Iran policy, the nuclear deal.

At one time the treaty was a good and rational idea. Many Iranians applauded its signing in 2015 because they associated it with the hope of a new openness in the country. But with the failure of all efforts towards reform, and the popular uprising, the circumstances have changed completely. A state that opens fire on its own people every day – every day! – will not be a reliable party to external treaties. An agreement now would not be worth the ink it is signed with. And it would cost the blood of peaceful demonstrators in Iran. The revenue it would bring to Iran would flow directly into the repressive agencies, which control a large part of the Iranian economy. That means the West would be helping to perpetuate a regime which is being severely destabilized domestically. Only a democratic development in Iran can lead to security, stability and access to the country's energy sources. But a nuclear deal would become the Nord Stream 2 of German and European Middle East policy. And this brings us back to Ukraine and the German president's speech.

Die Zeit, 15 December 2022

People say Mohsen Shekari wanted to become a stand-up comedian. He is said to have worked as a barista in a café in the busy Tehran district of Sattarkhan, to have loved the *God of War* video games and been very athletic; he was a fan of Bayern Munich. His brother, they say, is an engineer who earns his living as a driver for Snapp, the Iranian version of Uber – one of hundreds of thousands, millions of educated young people in Iran who work in low-paying jobs to make ends meet. His sister studied psychology and works as a receptionist in a doctor's office. There is nothing about his parents yet that I have seen. But I have seen his mother, standing beside some parked cars in an alley, a middle-aged woman with the knee-length coat and the loose headscarf which most Iranian women have been wearing for the past forty years in unwilling conformance with the dress code: in a video taken from above at a range of 50 to 80 metres, she presses her hands to her face, bends her torso back and forth, and cries horrific lamentations to heaven. Some older passers-by or relatives hurry to her side to quiet her and lead her away, but she is screaming so loud, Mohseeeen, Mohseeeen, that it must be audible throughout the neighbourhood. I understand that, a few seconds before, she learned that her son had been executed. Mohsen Shekari was twenty-three years old, and is the first Iranian to have been hanged for his participation in the current protests.

According to reports, on 25 September Mohsen observed, from the counter of his café, a crowd demonstrating against the murder of Jina Mahsa Amini. He went outside and shouted anti-government slogans too. Members of the paramilitary Basiji militia rode into the crowd on motorcycles, as they customarily do at smaller protests, the passengers on the back seats equipped with clubs, knives or pistols. One of the militiamen, it is said, dismounted from the motorcycle with his knife and attacked a young woman who had fallen in the open drainage ditch at the side of the road. Mohsen is supposed to have thrown himself on the militiaman so that the woman could escape but was then pulled down himself and kicked. When the militiaman left off to remount the motorcycle, Mohsen fetched a kitchen knife from his café. Returning to the street, he and other demonstrators built a blockade to fend off the next attack of the militiamen. When it came, Mohsen brandished his kitchen knife in great agitation towards a militiaman who was approaching him with a club. When the militiaman raised his club to bring it down on Mohsen, Mohsen reportedly stuck the knife in his belly. Blood spurted out; Mohsen was afraid he had killed or severely wounded the militiaman. He dropped the knife and stood weeping beside the militiaman. 'I only wanted him not to hit us,' he shouted again and again as they led him away, 'I only wanted him not to hit us.' He and other demonstrators had not yet seen that the wound was only superficial and was quickly treated.

Is all of this true? I do not know; I am only repeating the accounts of eyewitnesses and relatives that have been collected and placed online since Mohsen's execution so that his story may never be forgotten. And they seem to me all the more plausible as they do not deny that Mohsen wounded a militiaman. Not even the prosecution claims that a murder was committed; Mohsen was charged only with the attempt to kill a militiaman and was alleged to have been hired to do it by a third party. A mere attempted homicide would not be a capital offence, even under the Islamic Republic's penal code. But what is the use of talking about laws in a country that has never even attempted to hide its despotism. Of course Mohsen was not allowed to engage counsel in his defence, nor to read the evidence against him. In court, the kitchen knife became a machete, the minor stab wound in the belly became a serious wound in the shoulder which required thirteen stitches, the situation of self-defence became a conspiracy. Mohsen's uncle told *The Guardian* that his face showed clear marks of torture.

In Evin Prison, Mohsen Shekari is said to have joked with everyone. He was a simple, honest and somewhat credulous young man, according to a cellmate who was released from prison a few days ago. The cellmate admits that his last words to Mohsen were a scolding; he will never forgive himself for that. He wanted to sleep, but Mohsen was recounting a scene from a comedy show to the other prisoners in a lively voice, so he shouted at him to be quiet. Mohsen lay down, angry, and soon began snoring. His nose is said to have been broken during his arrest, so that he had trouble breathing. It was noon when the prison loudspeakers announced that Mohsen Shekari had been executed for 'corruption on earth and war against God'. The prisoners in Mohsen's cell stared in silence at the empty bunk over which the team photo of Bayern Munich still hung.

According to reports, Mohsen's parents were taken in by a lie on the part of the authorities: shortly before the execution, they received a call to say that Mohsen would be pardoned and they should therefore keep calm and in no case make any public statements. Their son would soon be released. They went to the prison in the hope of taking Mohsen in their arms. But, in fact, Mohsen was executed while his parents waited for news outside the prison; thus the video must have been shot last Thursday near Evin Prison. When their son's possessions were handed over to them, his parents were told that Mohsen had atoned for his sins by his death and could therefore be considered a Muslim again and buried in the public cemetery. His family would not be charged for his upkeep during his imprisonment. However, his uncle reported that the family was sent twice to different cemeteries for their son's burial. Each time, they were told when they arrived there that their son's body was somewhere else. This is 'the usual game, to torment the family some more,' Mohsen's uncle said.

More than 18,000 participants in the anti-government protests are said to be in prison by now, and the Iranian parliament has demanded that they too be convicted of 'war against God', which carries a mandatory death sentence under Iranian law. There is no doubt that the Islamic Republic has no scruples against executing thousands of political prisoners within days, or a few weeks; it has done so before, immediately after the revolution and again in 1988. But this time something is different. This time, every one of the people executed has a face – as does the 23-year-old amateur wrestler Majidreza Rahnavard, for example, who wore wire-rimmed glasses and long hair like John Lennon's. In one of the photos, he is casually straddling a motorcycle whose front wheel is suspended in the air. He was arrested on 19 November at a demonstration in Mashhad and sentenced to death just five days later. Just a few days ago, Majidreza's mother is said to have received permission to visit him. She left the prison happy because she had been given to understand that her son would soon be released. Pictures from the prison posted online show mother and son hugging and smiling into the camera. On Monday, when she went to visit Majidreza again, his mother was told that he had been hanged in the morning and had already been buried.

It is evident that the Leader of the Revolution Khamenei, after initial hesitation, has decided to use brute force to stay in power. After the most recent escalation, he can hardly turn back; his political fate, and possibly his life, depends on the security forces repressing the protests. Is that still possible? With every execution, the horror spreads, and even employees of the system are more and more often dissociating themselves from it in public. Last week, Khamenei's sister disowned him; the arch-conservative former director of the state broadcasting network, Mohammed Sarafraz, had called on the leader of the revolution to reverse course as early as 22 November. Sarafraz was appointed by Khamenei personally and has been on the sanctions list of the European Union for years because of coerced confessions on Iranian television and other human rights violations. The violence against the Iranian people will bring the Islamic Republic to a dead end sooner or later, Sarafraz says in a video communiqué: 'I am aware that anything can happen to me after these words, so I have made my will.'

Meanwhile the authorities have published the names of twenty-two more condemned prisoners who are to be hanged soon. Even now, the stories are being collected which will one day take their place in the hagiography of Iranian martyrs. The well-known radiologist Hamid Ghare-Hassanlou and his wife Farzaneh are among them; the stage actor Hossein Mohammed and the professional footballer Amir Nasr-Azadani. The list also includes three minors, Arin Farzamnia, Amin Mehdi Shokrollahi and Amir Mehdi Jaffari. The next to be executed is supposed to be the 22-year-old Mahan Sadrat, who persistently refused in court to confess that he had had a knife with him, much less wounded a security officer. According to reports, his execution has already been ordered. Many more mothers in Iran will cry their children's names to heaven. Remembering them, every single one of them, everywhere in the country, preserves the hope of freedom in the future of Iran.